MAN VERSUS SOCIETY IN EIGHTEENTH-CENTURY BRITAIN

SIX POINTS OF VIEW

MAN VERSUS SOCIETY
IN EIGHTEENTH-CENTURY
BRITAIN

SIX POINTS OF VIEW

J. H. PLUMB, JACOB VINER, G. R. CRAGG
RUDOLF WITTKOWER, PAUL HENRY LANG
BERTRAND H. BRONSON

EDITED BY
JAMES L. CLIFFORD

The Norton Library
W · W · NORTON & COMPANY · INC ·
NEW YORK

First published in the Norton Library 1972
by arrangement with Cambridge University Press

Books That Live
The Norton imprint on a book means that in the publisher's
estimation it is a book not for a single season but for the years.
W. W. Norton & Company, Inc.

First published 1968
Reprinted by permission of Cambridge University Press

SBN   393   00608   5

CONTENTS

ACKNOWLEDGMENTS

The symposium here recorded, which was held on 14–16 October 1966, was sponsored by the Conference on British Studies in conjunction with the University of Delaware and the Henry Francis du Pont Winterthur Museum. Thanks are due to all who contributed to make it a success—to Dr J. Jean Hecht, who made the first suggestion; to Professor Calhoun Winton, who served as a most effective liaison between the Conference, the University, and the Winterthur Museum; to President John Perkins and Dean Arnold Lippert of the University, for their gracious invitation to Newark, Delaware; to Mr Charles van Ravenswaay, the Director of the Winterthur Museum and to Dr E. McClung Fleming, Director of the Education Division, for their memorable hospitality; and to all those at the University whose efficiency and quiet dedication made the arrangements for the symposium flawless, in particular Mrs Sara Mačuga, Secretary of the Winterthur Program, Mr Donald Bard, Coordinator of Conferences, and Professor Anthony Loudis of the Music Department.

The committee who arranged the programme was made up of Professor James L. Clifford, Chairman, Dr James M. Osborn, Professor Robert Walcott, Professor Calhoun Winton, and Dr Louis B. Wright. Valuable help was given by Professor Donald Grove Barnes, President of the Conference on British Studies, and by Professor Ruth Emery, Executive Secretary.

Pertinent remarks of some of the principal commentators are quoted in the summary at the end of this volume.

J. L. C.

PREFACE

The eighteenth century, perhaps more than any other period, has suffered at the hands of labellers. 'The Age of Reason', 'The Age of Elegance', 'The Neoclassical Age', 'The Enlightenment'—all these sound plausible, but give a false impression of uniformity and cohesiveness. Scholars are more skeptical today about the validity of such labels, since increasing factual knowledge and critical relativism have brought deeper awareness of the complexity of all historical periods. As a result, generalisations formerly accepted without question are now regarded less as truisms than as myths to be knocked down.

The attacks, to be sure, have generally come from specialists in particular fields—from literary critics using examples of writers who do not appear to fit, from historians using parliamentary alignments and election results, or from students of architecture tracing Palladian enthusiasms or Gothic revivals. It has been rare to find simultaneous assault from diverse disciplines. Yet this is just what is needed. If overall generalisations have any justification whatsoever they must prove their applicability to many different fields of endeavour.

In any discussion of the matter certain questions keep recurring. What opportunity in the eighteenth century did the individual have for self-realisation? From an abundance of evidence we can guess what life was like for geniuses like Pope or Swift, or William Pitt or Burke, or Handel or Sir Joshua Reynolds. But what of the average man in the various arts and professions? How did he fare in the economy of his time? And what of the poor and uneducated? What were the social and cultural pressures which limited or checked a man's desires to live fully? This set of questions is difficult to answer.

An intriguing test suggested itself. Why not arrange a special interdisciplinary symposium, with eighteenth-century Britain as its general subject? A group of experts in widely divergent fields might be set to examine some intentionally general theme, such as 'Man versus Society in Eighteenth-Century Britain'—one which would cut across various aspects of life of the time and transcend the boundaries of present-day scholarly routines. What would they say? With no coaching or obvious attempts at unifying the approach, how would leading authorities in history, economics, religion, fine arts, music and literature—to choose six major disciplines—answer the challenge? Is it possible that there would be any uniformity in their reactions? Or would each attack the problem independently and arrive at completely different results? What follows in this volume provides the answer. Here is what six outstanding authorities have to say on this provocative topic.

CHAPTER I

POLITICAL MAN

by J. H. Plumb

Most of the cultural and intellectual activities of Englishmen in the
eighteenth century enjoyed an extension of public participation—
art, music, literature, as well as theology, philosophy and history
reached deeper into the nation: books, magazines, pamphlets,
newspapers tumbled from the presses; and certainly there were far
more literate men and women, aware of the great issues of the day,
than there had been. Did, however, the political life of the nation
run counter to this general development? Was the individual
excluded more and more from political activity by the extension
of the life of parliament from three to seven years, by the decline
of party, and by the growth of oligarchy? A narrow view of
politics, a myopic concentration on the mechanics of parliamentary elections, might lead one to believe so, but politics and
political issues still reached beyond the confines of Westminster.
They were of paramount interest to a nation whose liberties, no
matter how oddly institutionalised, were the object of envious
admiration among the liberal philosophers of Western Europe.
Consider for a moment the fury unleashed by the Excise Bill, or
by the attempt to permit Jewish Naturalisation or even by the
Cider Tax: to say nothing of Wilkes, America and the rest, and
one cannot doubt the widespread participation of Englishmen in
politics. True these outbursts were partly engineered, and they
were but tornadoes that swept the surface, for the basic structure
of eighteenth-century politics was very stable, steel-like in its
strength, even if it bent in the wind. The political experience of
the seventeenth century was not obliterated over night, either by

the Glorious Revolution or the Septennial Act: radicals and Tories existed even in 1750. Politics was never merely a matter for the politicians.

In the seventeenth century in order to win their victories against the Crown, the gentry and their aristocratic allies had called into being a large parliamentary electorate, and one which from time to time exercised the powers of choice. Between 1700 and 1715, eight general elections for parliament were held, a far greater number than have ever been held since in a comparable time-span. Also, during this period only a handful of parliamentary boroughs avoided a contest, even those with very small electorates.[1]

In order to understand the relationship of the individual to the political institutions by which he was governed in the eighteenth century, it is very necessary to look at this early period more closely, for it deeply influenced all subsequent political history of the Hanoverian period.

There are a number of elementary factors to remember about politics in the reign of Queen Anne which are sometimes overlooked. One I have already mentioned, the exceptional frequency of general elections, and, at these elections, contests in all types of constituency were rarely avoided for more than an election or two. Counties went very frequently to a poll, involving, except in such tiny counties as Rutland, thousands of freeholders. Some counties where divisions went very deep, such as Essex, were fought time and time again. As with the counties, so with the great boroughs: Westminster, Bristol, Norwich, Coventry and their like were battle grounds for—and I have no hesitation in using the word—party. Nor did the tiny boroughs avoid contests: a few did, but even some of the smallest corporations possessed their party divisions, and often the defection of one or two voters could swing the town from a Whig to a Tory patron. Frequent elections, contests and party, Whigs versus Tories—these are the three major ingredients of the politics of this period: factors which enabled most gentlemen and a number of freeholders and burgesses to exercise a free political choice.[1] And this was England's vast singularity, a unique situation amongst the major powers of the world at this time.

The issues were clear, and understood by thousands of voters, if not all, and men in the heart of borough politics watched closely and with passion what was happening at Westminster. The choice of the Speaker of the House of Commons in 1705 was a vital test of party strength: John Smith was supported by the Whigs and the Court, William Bromley by the Tories.[2] Smith got home, in spite of a defection of seventeen Tory placemen to Bromley. (They paid for such insubordination later when fifteen of them lost their places.)[3] The contest had been avidly followed back in King's Lynn by Robert Walpole's Whig supporters. One of the leaders of the Lynn Whigs wrote off at once: 'the Choice of your Speaker is very pleasing to all honest men, but on the contrary a great Mortification to the High Church papists and atheists.'[4]

It was not only the great issues that these local politicians watched: they were keenly aware of the twists and turns of party tactics. Another Turner, John, the nephew of Charles, and Robert Walpole's least inhibited supporter in Lynn, wrote to him on 7 December 1705

I cannot tell what to judge of your condition when last Votes I saw[5] you were outmustered by 29 in the Agmondisham election.[6] I never thought to find Sr Edward Seymour [the Tory leader] a prophett, as our parsons will certainly represent him to be, for they encourage themselves with a saying of his that 205 volunteers will beat 248 prest men, so they still think to get the better of you.[7] But I cannot see they misse a man and I am sure you had a great many absent but if they will not apeare, they ought to be reckoned as cyphers. If you were not more hearty yesterday, I expect to heare you are baulkt at Norwich too.[8]

Politics mattered. And the number of people involved was very considerable. Take Norwich, which worried John Turner. In 1705, about 2,500 men voted: probably about 25 per cent of the active male population, and only 150 votes separated the Whig and Tory candidates. The principles were clear-cut: on the part of the Whigs support for Marlborough's war (Turner had been terrified that there might be a reverse before the election), and opposition to the High Church party; dislike of high taxes, dissenters and courtiers on the part of the Tories.

Throughout the land, the electorate was divided. Small boroughs or large counties were both prone to attacks of party fever. So long as the Tories had prospects of office, their guineas could ring as true as a Whig's: in the pressure of circumstances, doubtful voters, wobblers uncertain of their own or the world's future, could float one way, then another, and often upset the certainties of machine politics. This is why, on occasion, the influence of Lord Wharton in quite small boroughs snapped and he found his candidates defeated and Tories returned. So long as power could come to the Tories—and it could and did for most of Queen Anne's reign, the factors which made for political stability —bribery and influence combined with open voting—were kept in check. Politics remained a game for two players.

Issues therefore counted; the gentry, who were very numerous, were divided sharply on questions of war and peace, on toleration of dissent and the succession to the Crown, matters which Elizabeth I thought should be reserved for princes. In Queen Anne's reign they were questions for the electorate, a remarkable development in a hundred years. But, of course, they were not the only questions. Politics have always been more than a question of issues: they imply the pursuit of power. By 1700, politicians were well aware that the freedom of the electorate could be a stumbling-block in their quest for power. Already determined and successful efforts had been made to eradicate party strife in the constituencies and to reduce them to subordination. Every art was used to secure control. Of course, there was much variety. Sometimes the personal, patriarchal and traditional authority of a great family, not necessarily very rich or very generous, was sufficient to dominate the small parliamentary borough that nestled against its estate: such was the authority of the Rashleighs at Fowey, the Burrards of Lymington or the Leighs of Lyme. But such corporations were getting rare by 1700. Most voters, no matter how loyal to a person or a party, knew that they possessed, in their parliamentary franchise, negotiable currency. Many of them liked to turn it into hard cash.

There has been too much evasion of the question of bribery: money played its part throughout the eighteenth century. Indeed, expenses steadily grew, particularly after the Septennial Act of 1716, which gave a seven years instead of a three years return on the investment. At Weobley in Herefordshire voters expected a minimum of £5 and often secured £20. And, as ever with bribery, they sometimes took money from both sides, but this was a dangerous practice when voting was open and gentlemen could break a mere tradesman's head with impunity. But bribery, like rich and lavish entertainment, seems to have been endemic in certain boroughs. Weobley, until most of the vote-houses were bought up, had a very bad name; so had Stockbridge and Great Bedwyn, where the poor weavers got what they could whilst the going was good. At Coventry, however, it was all drink, food and riot, usually organised by the innkeepers, that made its elections some of the most lurid of the eighteenth century. But it is as well to remember Coventry, along with Westminster, Middlesex and elsewhere, for they demonstrate that eighteenth-century politics could be savage and brutal with mobs roaring and rioting through the streets. Nor, as we shall see, was this violence necessarily confined to election times: political crisis too could unleash violence, and permit the individual to assuage his hatred of a system that more and more excluded him from power.[1]

But the political world of the Augustans did not consist merely in venal or riotous boroughs. Half the members of parliament came from boroughs with moderate or small electorates. Until the total defeat of the Tory party in 1715 and its obliteration from the serious world of politics, these boroughs were often very difficult to manage. Even small electorates, such as that of Buckingham, which only numbered thirteen, could be touchy. They expected entertainment; that was the *sine qua non* of politics throughout the century: a voter looked forward to gigantic binges at the candidates' or patrons' expense, not only at elections but also on other corporate occasions, such as the election of a mayor. They required more solid pledges: plate to adorn their guildhalls, schools and charities for their sons, water supplies to save themselves the expense, but, above all, jobs. The letter-bag of every M.P. with the slightest pretensions to influence was stuffed with pleas and demands from voters for themselves, their relations or their dependants. Places in the Customs and Excise, in the Army and Navy, in the Church, in the East India, Africa and Levant Companies, in all the departments of state from door-keepers to clerks: jobs at Court for the real gentry or sinecures in Ireland, the diplomatic corps, or anywhere else where duties were light and salaries steady. These were the true coin of politics, the solvent that diminished or obliterated principle. And they worked faster once the Tory party had no hope of power. This was apparent to the meanest intelligence by the 1730s when Boling-broke finally threw in his hand and retired to France.[1]

Naturally with places comparatively scarce there were always more applicants than jobs, and this led the political managers to attempt to get rid of the electorate when they could, or discipline it when they could not. At first this may not have been a conscious process, but it rapidly became one.

In the small corporations the elimination of unwanted voters became a process of steady attrition: freemen, if they had the vote, ceased to be made, or the fee for admission to the freehold was pushed beyond the pocket of the small tradesman. In others, honorary freemen, usually reliable gentry from the surrounding countryside, were made in order to swing the electorate at the appropriate moment. More often than not, in an election disputed on petition, the House of Commons came down heavily on the side of the narrower franchise. To make the question of franchise more certain and therefore more manageable, the House passed in 1729 the Last Determinations Act, by which franchises were frozen to the last decision of the House on the question. Where votes went with property, it was bought up, at excessive cost maybe at the time, but future expensive contests could be eliminated. At Weobley in Herefordshire the electorate was quickly reduced from about 150 to 45 by such means.

Corporations with large electorates and the county constituencies posed different problems. Some voters in both types of constituency were controllable. It was rare, although not unknown, for a tenant to disobey his landlord and vote against his wishes; mostly they did as they were told. Nor could craftsmen be expected to disoblige rich and powerful merchant aldermen living in their wards. Voting was open, and in these large constituencies it became common after 1700 for votes to be printed after the election in order that they could be analysed.[1] And, of course, there were loyalties—familial, territorial and political. Then, as now, men were born into the politics which they professed. All of this gave cohesion—at least to parties—but they did not diminish the enmity between them, whether these parties were political or factional or a mixture of both, particularly at a time when the gentry were both numerous and sharply divided. But contests in large constituencies became ruinously expensive, particularly after the Septennial Act of 1716.[2] In large counties such as Yorkshire with a numerous gentry, subscriptions could make even an expensive fight feasible, but, in smaller counties, the cost grew too high, so in county after county a treaty was made. Men sank their differences—the aristocracy sometimes taking one seat for a Whig, the gentry the other for a Tory: occasionally the gentry got both: in other counties the representation was divided geographically. After 1734 county contests became exceptionally infrequent. Twelve counties were not contested between 1754 and 1790, fifteen only once, so that it was a rare freeholder who exercised a vote more than once in his lifetime, and thousands never had even that one chance.[1] A marked contrast with the period between 1688 and 1725 when county elections were exceptionally common, and freeholders voted time and time again.

Hence, by the middle decades of the eighteenth century, a diminished electorate functioned only intermittently—with regularity at all elections only in about fifteen constituencies of which three, oddly enough, were in Kent.[2] Elsewhere contests were uncommon, often twenty years or more elapsing without a contest. Hence, the individual who possessed a political franchise very rarely had the opportunity to exercise it. Political power, both local and national, had been absorbed by groups of political managers whose ambitions, of course, varied as much as their own natures, but self-interest loomed larger than political principle. Indeed, principles might have died a total death but for the fact that the parliamentary system never became completely closed or the public without influence.

Politics, fortunately, are more than a matter of elections and the exercise of a franchise. Men were touched in their daily lives; often indeed knocked down by them. Although the volume of eighteenth-century legislation, in a public sense, was small; its private legislation was immense: and the eighteenth-century gentleman set about making a world to his own liking. Commercialisation of agriculture had begun centuries before, but the pace became headlong in the eighteenth century, which witnessed the near-elimination of the peasantry as a class. Enclosure bills rattled through the Commons. They were hated: throughout the country, the peasantry rioted against them. In 1710 the villagers rose at Bedingfield and the Norfolk Militia had to be called out to put them down.[3] Turnpikes were no better loved but they proliferated. The birds of the air, the rabbits of the heath, the fish in the streams were ferociously protected for the sport and sustenance of gentlemen. Property acquired the sanctity of life and theft meant death. Benefit of clergy was abolished and hanging as a punishment for crime increased.[1] Trivial crimes might mean transportation for life, first to America and then, after the Revolution, to Australia. The gentlemen merchants who ran the towns did not neglect themselves. In the 1760s and 1770s enabling acts permitted them to charge rates for many public services—paving, lighting, even police—which they supplied, although without notable efficiency. Politics was power, not only for individuals who manned the pumps and sluices of the parliamentary system, but also for the class which had come to dominate British life—commercially minded landowners with a sharp eye for profit.

In the earlier decades of the century the strains of the agrarian revolution had caused divisions within the landowning class; indeed this is the social basis of the cleavage between Whig and Tory, but the plight of the smaller gentry, still subject to vicissitude, had gradually eased and by the middle of the century a golden era was opening for them. This too helped to give solidity to the political system, which by 1750 had acquired a seemingly adamantine strength. What was increasingly obvious to the world at large was the development of a self-gratifying oligarchy that held power for its own profit.

The political nation, however, was always greater than those involved in the parliamentary system. It was growing throughout the eighteenth century both in size and in economic and social importance, and this aspect of politics was not affected by the setback of the Tory party. The seventeenth century, particularly its three periods of violent political struggle—the Civil War and Protectorate, the Exclusion Crisis and the Revolution of 1688—had accustomed literate Englishmen to controversy: pamphlets, ballads, books were all used to influence political passion or to convince by argument. And the spread of the coffee house—viewed with alarm by Charles II and his ministers—had created, along with bookshops, not only centres for the dissemination of literature but also meeting grounds for men passionately interested in politics. Political literature spread to the provinces, to the country houses, to the taverns and inns of large country towns: provincial bookshops were more common than historians have allowed (after all, think of Johnson's father): the citizens of London were not the only clubbable Englishmen: King's Lynn had a flourishing Whig dining club by Queen Anne's reign, if not before. By the time of Swift's first political pamphlet, there was a wide literate public, willing to spend its sixpence on a good piece of invective and to spread the copy around amongst like-minded neighbours.

Nor did this public diminish after 1715; indeed it grew: the public grew as the electorate diminished. The success of the *Craftsman* was due entirely to its existence. True, the usual edition of the *Craftsman* was only about 3,000, and not infrequently below that figure; but issues which caught the public's attention soared to 6,000 and may have reached, on one or two occasions, 10,000.[1] And each copy was read by far more people than would read a present-day weekly. We know that the *Craftsman* was in great demand in the provinces.[2] But the *Craftsman* was but one paper, and there were many others from *Fog's Weekly* to the *London Evening Post* that were equally concerned with politics. And the newspaper was not the only means of propaganda. Pantomime, harlequinades, burlesques, Punch and Judy shows were given political twists. The London stage has never been more dominated by politics than it was between 1725 and 1737 when, slandered beyond endurance, Walpole instituted a censorship of the theatre.[3] Whether he had a chance to vote or not, the literate and semi-literate Englishman had plenty of opportunity to jeer and scoff at his rulers. And at a more serious level he was exceptionally well informed.

Furthermore there was something of a cultural explosion in the middle decades of the eighteenth century, when literacy increased by leaps and bounds. Because of the decay of Oxford and Cambridge and some of the old-established grammar schools, there has been too ready an acceptance of the view that these years witnessed not only stagnation but retrogression in education. But schools were sprouting like mushrooms. Primarily they were started to provide elementary commercial training for boys, a veneer of middle-class polish for girls, and of course a fortune for the schoolmaster. As so frequently in eighteenth-century life, the fee was often more important than the service and schools could vanish overnight.[1] Nevertheless, many were good and stable. Something of the extent of this development may be assessed from the fact that 100 schools, most of them newly established, advertised in the *Northampton Mercury* between 1720 and 1760, and, even more impressive, the *Norwich Mercury* advertised sixty-three schools between 1749 and 1756.[2] And, a point which requires very little labouring, there was now a provincial press to advertise in. By 1760 there were forty provincial newspapers established in all the major towns of England. And, of course, the papers were not confined to the towns they were printed in—an elaborate system of itinerant pedlars, who often travelled forty or fifty miles in a day, disseminated them throughout the land. The *Northampton Mercury* was on sale in Sheffield, Cambridge, Warwick and Oxford—indeed throughout the East and West Midlands. Similarly the *Stamford Mercury* travelled up and down the Great North Road with the stage coaches.[3]

This new and growing literate public was also politically active. One has only to turn over the pages of Cowburne's *Liverpool Chronicle* for 1768 to discover that it is alive with political debate—letters urging freeholders how to vote in the coming general election, political information from Ireland and America, and curiously enough Wilkes's fortunes in the Middlesex election were avidly followed, the sympathies of the paper being entirely with Wilkes. Fifty or sixty years previously there had been no such politically minded public in Liverpool: indeed there was not a public sufficient to run a newspaper, let alone two. There had been politicians, Whigs and Tories, a corporation well aware of political issues and a few hundred freeholders of varying political independence who were not unaware of the great issues at stake at Westminster, but now politics in Liverpool had moved into a different dimension. There were now thousands, not hundreds, of men and women alive to political issues and keen to debate them, even though they had no vote.[1]

The same was true not only of large and growing towns such as Liverpool, Bristol, Newcastle or Hull, but also of a new class of men and their skilled workers who were beginning to plant industry not in towns, but in the English countryside. Josiah Wedgwood at Etruria followed politics as keenly as his partner Thomas Bentley followed fashion in London.[2] And Jedediah Strutt over at Belper kept his eye on the political scene in London.[3] And, when the supporters in Middlesex of Wilkes are analysed, what do we find? The bulk of them are middling people—traders, craftsmen, petty manufacturers, men of small property.[4] Here was the public for whom Tom Paine was to write. His *Rights of Man* entranced Wedgwood. Here, indeed, is a political nation whom Namier and his followers have almost entirely ignored: as essential a part of the structure of politics at the accession of George III as the Cornish boroughs or the Shropshire gentlemen. Evidence of the political nation's size and vigour everywhere abounds. These are the people who roared for Chatham and hissed George III, who subscribed for comforts for American prisoners of British forces, who read and studied Paine, Priestley, Price and Cartwright. Were there then two worlds of politics in the eighteenth century—a tight political establishment, linked to small groups of powerful political managers in the provinces, who controlled parliament, the executive and all that was effective in the nation, and outside this an amorphous mass of political sentiment that found expression in occasional hysteria and impotent polemic, but whose effective voice in the nation was negligible?

Actually the political nation and the political establishment had never been completely divorced. Their relations certainly were strained and their contacts intermittent, but they existed. For one thing contests in the populous boroughs and counties sometimes took place and when they did more than the actual voters took part: mobs, processions, addresses and the like made those active at the hustings conscious of the popular will on political issues and those free from the strait-jacket of direct influence could be swayed by a sense of what they felt the nation wanted. Undoubtedly the enormous popular sympathy for Wilkes amongst the lower and middling classes affected those freeholders of the eastern and urban districts of Middlesex that were less prone to the influence of a landlord.

And there were Addresses. The right of a county or a corporation to address parliament was age-old. Although in the middle decades of the century the Commons was dominated by a single party, it was factionalised, and in the 1760s the factions were often at loggerheads on political issues of importance—America and Wilkes: later there were even more issues—reform of parliament, slave trade, Ireland, even commerce with France. Issues, *pace* Namier, abounded. And they divided counties and corporations. The Excise Bills even in 1733 had set the country aflame and Addresses rained on parliament.[1] During the War of American Independence the situation was equally intense. Again from the letters of Josiah Wedgwood we see how sharply Staffordshire was divided: some willing to support George III and Lord North in their intransigence, others driven frantic by it, and both sides addressing parliament from totally opposite standpoints in the name of the county as a whole. Such Addresses were usually initiated at a so-called meeting of the county—gentlemen, substantial freeholders, office holders and Church dignitaries, that is men who belonged to the official political establishment. But they needed the political nation to back them, so Addresses required signatures and we know that copies were left in local taverns where men were solicited to sign. Such solicitations could only lead to argument and discussion and to a widening of political horizons. At Westminster, Addresses, except loyal ones, had very little effect, but they helped, perhaps, to moderate political passion. In the provinces they brought like-minded men into greater cohesion, and made them realise something of their own importance.

So by the 1760s there existed, in effect, two political nations in England, one growing, the other shrinking, with little contact between them. Had there been more, the grosser follies of handling both Wilkes and America could scarcely have taken place. The formal electorate was dwindling and called to execute its judgment less and less. Those who by education and interest might reasonably expect a political voice but were denied it, were steadily increasing. There were other factors, too, at work to help widen this cleavage: the dissenters. For decades their leaders had hoped against hope that their civic disabilities would be removed. Many, but by no means all, now felt that only a radical reform of political institutions could bring this about. Much of the aggressive criticism of parliament in the second half of the century came from dissent.[1]

Again in 1763, over twenty years of war came to an end. That war had been commercially aggressive: 'Commerce', in the words of Burke, 'had been made to flourish through war': both patriotism and profit had helped to still the voice of criticism. The dislocations of peace, however, combined with what seemed to many merchants a wanton return to France of commercial privileges seized during the war, helped to breed discontent. That is why they received George III at the Guildhall in stony silence. Demobilisation and unemployment added yeast to the dough. And, for once, the professional politicians were in need of public issues. George III was young and there were no prospects of succession. Hence there were no 'futures' for them to dabble in. Some, like the duke of Newcastle, had played the 'in game' for so long that rousing the public had no charms for them, but Chatham possessed no inhibitions, and even Burke saw the necessity of exploiting the American grievances on behalf of the Rockinghams. Public protest, so long as it was skilfully handled, acquired a certain attraction for the Venetian oligarchy: they could now find a personal use for public discontent. It was the fusion of these circumstances which helped to create some of the great political debates of the 1760s and 1770s and provided Chatham, Wilkes and Junius with their opportunities. The political establishment might ignore Wilkes and only give America a modicum of its attention, but it could not remain absolutely impervious to the criticisms and claims of the wider political nation. After all, John Wilkes did win his battle with parliament. Nor could the oligarchy remain deaf to threats to itself.

The demand for parliamentary reform in the 1770s and 1780s developed primarily in the towns. Even in the 1760s the Liverpool Debating Society was arguing whether politics could ever be purified without the introduction of the ballot box. It was the exclusion from the political power which they felt was rightly theirs because of their social and economic activity that led men such as Josiah Wedgwood to support annual parliaments, universal suffrage and the control of a member's actions by his constituents. The growing criticism of parliament as an institution swelled to a gale in the late seventies as disaster after disaster dogged North's American policies. It was not only the unrepresentative nature of Parliament which came in for the fury of attack, but also the graft which the political establishment lavished on itself. This new radicalism covered numerous shades of opinion from republican to Tory. Historians, I feel, never give sufficient emphasis to the prevalence of bitter anti-monarchical, pro-republican sentiment of the 1760s and 1770s. Sylas Neville's diary and papers demonstrate clearly enough that in the provinces, as well as in London, there were many men and women who were enthusiastic supporters of republican ideas, with strong sympathies towards

America, men and women who possessed as much hatred of George III as the most dedicated Boston radicals. After all, Neville never had the slightest difficulty in collecting a few cronies on 30 January to toast the execution of Charles I.[1] And Tom Paine's books, it must be remembered, sold in far greater quantities than those of any other political commentator. Indeed Paine and his readership cry aloud for further investigation.

This powerful radicalism was strongest in London, the big seaport towns and the growing manufacturing districts of Lancashire, the West Midlands and the West Riding of Yorkshire, but it combined with, and indeed was itself infused with, the ideas of the Tory radicalism of the earlier decades of the century which had called, not for fundamental reform, but for the purification of political institutions. The country-squire's old panacea of annual parliaments and the exclusion of placemen from parliament acquired in the hands of the Reverend Christopher Wyvill and the Yorkshire Association fresh vigour. Even their suggestion that the number of Knights of the Shire should be increased in order to strengthen the independent element in parliament was no novelty. It had been adumbrated in the first year of the century.[2]

There is no need here to trace the course of the first strong movement for parliamentary reform or even to discuss whether or not this brought England to the very edge of revolution. For my purpose it is enough to indicate the width of political interest and to underline the conflict which existed between the political establishment and the political nation: a conflict which did not begin with Junius or end with the failure of the Association movement. Its origins lie in the seventeenth-century emergence of the electorate and the division was not healed until the late nineteenth century, for the growth of the political nation was always far faster than the spread of representative government. What are of interest, in the context of this paper, in the last two decades of the eighteenth century are two developments. One is the even more rapid growth of the political nation which began to acquire new leadership and a more sophisticated organisation, and the effect of patriotism in helping the establishment defeat its aspirations. Nor were these two factors dissociated. Fears for property proved a strong stimulant to loyalty.

Interest in politics penetrated deeper into society during the last two decades of the eighteenth century, although in London, at least, political interest amongst the working classes may have been more extensive than historians have allowed. A Swiss traveller, César de Saussure, was highly amused in 1726 to see shoe-blacks reading newspapers for the foreign news.[1] And craftsmen were well aware that parliament's legislation affected their interests— usually adversely.[2] By 1750 what was essentially a lower-middle-class debating society—the Robin Hood (well-named)—had achieved notoriety. There were a number of deist and political clubs operating in a twilight world of mechanics and intellectuals. The part played by the humbler freemasons in starting and main-taining such clubs, which were partly educational as well as political, needs investigating, but the connection may be close. After all, Thomas Hardy was an active member of the pseudo-masonic organisation called the Gregorians.[3] Lower-middle-class radicalism grew during the 1780s and 1790s and received further impetus from the early phases of the French Revolution. Tom Paine's *Rights of Man* is reputed to have sold 400,000 copies, a prodigious figure, even allowing for a considerable margin of error.[4] And contemporaries were quick to notice who was reading it. 'Our peasantry now read the *Rights of Man* on mountains and moors and by the wayside' wrote T. J. Mathias in 1797.[5] Radicalism was getting out of hand. The expensive books and pamphlets of Priestley and Price, the dilettante leadership of Horne Tooke, Major Cartwright, Earl Stanhope and the like could be tolerated, but Thomas Hardy's organisation was beginning to take on the unwelcome air of a revolutionary movement of *sans-culottes*. And the example of France was not beguiling. The solid bourgeois wing of the political nation read its Burke and drew far closer to the political establishment in sentiment. It did not want revolution; nevertheless it still desired power. So it entered into a more direct competition with the oligarchy over seats in parliament. After 1790 contested elections begin to increase rapidly again, and the cost of elections soared to new heights. There was a definite push by the richer commercial and manufacturing interests to buy their way into political power. Few such men as Beckford, Townsend or Sawbridge, city millionaires who supported Wilkes, were to be found consorting with the aggressive radical movement that took Paine for its hero. The French Revolution did not only close the ranks of the professional politicians. It did more than this. It drove deep fissures into the political nation itself. Whereas in the 1770s reform had not seemed to threaten property or status, it now reeked of revolution. As politics became national, they sharpened class division. And the terrible spectacle of a literate, politically minded, working class began to stalk the land. But it is not only the French Revolution that added a fresh dimension to the complexities of politics, divided as they were into this twofold world of political establishment and political nation. Patriotism became an issue as well as property.[1]

Of course patriotism is a highly complex matter, involving self-interest, aggressive economic appetites, xenophobia and a host of disreputable and semi-disreputable motives; it is a singularly powerful emotion. However, I am concerned not with causes, but with effects. We can see patriotism influencing radicalism in the later stages of the American War of Independence. Support for America had been very widespread in both London and the provinces, but, as soon as the American war became a general war, involving France and Spain, that support began to wither. Bristol, from being pro-American, became pro Lord North.[2] Even that ardent supporter of all things American, Josiah Wedgwood, began to have his doubts. If victory for America meant defeat of Britain by France and Spain, he was not at all sure that he could face such an outcome and he felt that he might have to support North. Although his radicalism remained firm, he was confused and baffled by the issues which *patriotism in the time of war* raised.[1] And, of course, the long wars against Revolutionary France and Napoleon in which armies were lost, invasion threatened and hundreds of ships sunk, posed a graver threat. It enabled Pitt and his supporters to denigrate radicalism as Jacobin, alien, anti-patriotic. In other countries—America, Russia, China—radical attitudes to society have joined with patriotism and been immensely strengthened by it. In England radicalism was seriously weakened first by the American War of Independence and afterwards by the wars against France.

By the end of the eighteenth century, the political nation had grown until it had begun to embrace some of the lowest classes of society. The true working class, however, that is the unskilled labourers in town and countryside, were, in spite of Tom Paine, still largely outside politics. They were stirring: increasingly they were beginning to realise that their condition in life depended on the political institutions by which they were governed and the men who ran them. The threat of a possible fusion between the lower middle classes and the working population, inspired by revolutionary ideas of political and social justice, spurred the richer leaders of the political nation and the political establishment to find a *modus vivendi*.

The division between the two, which had steadily grown during the eighteenth century, was, however, still deep in 1800. Provincial bankers and merchants, men such as Pares and Biggs of Leicester, felt that they lacked power both locally and nationally commensurate with their social and economic status. So long as such men did so, there was always a danger of a revolutionary situation. But they were as terrified as Hannah More of a politically conscious proletariat, and between 1800 and 1832 they fought their way into power through the old methods of the establishment—money and the unreformed system of parliamentary representation.[1] By the 1820s, some of the old-established conservative forces were losing the battle and running short of cash: for example, Leicester corporation, a bulwark of traditional oligarchy, had to mortgage its estates in 1826 to fight off the radical threat to its parliamentary representation. By 1831 it could not afford the money necessary to outbid the Leicester manufacturers who clubbed together to get their reform candidates in.[2] This was a far safer method of prising open the gates of political power than manning the barricades. The Reform Bill of 1832 marks the realignment of political forces: the powerful and rich leaders of the political nation, men who had used public issues and public agitation, forced the old political oligarchy to accommodate them—at a price. The old landowning and farming interests were strengthened by the large increase in the county membership. Politics remained, as it had been since the middle of the eighteenth century, an affair of two nations. But, as in the eighteenth century, they were not divorced: those who controlled the political machinery were susceptible to opinion. Europe was to give them lesson after lesson of the folly of ignoring the political hopes and aspirations of the mass of the people: and Britain's increasing riches permitted the extension of franchise without undue fear for the traditional institutions. So a process begun in the seventeenth century, and only temporarily checked in the eighteenth, was brought to fruition in the nineteenth. The process was the spread of politics to embrace the entire population. It was done with such skill that the conservative forces continued to dominate English life in spite of universal suffrage. Not until 1945 did Britain have a really radical government.

The eighteenth century opened with a large parliamentary electorate accustomed to exercising its powers; it was divided and organised into parties that were separated by sharp political issues. The total collapse of the Tories after 1715 permitted the development of oligarchy which both diminished and disciplined this electorate, although never to the point of extinction. This process was counterbalanced by a steady growth in the political consciousness of the nation at large, and by the development of strong economic and social interests that demanded political power. And the conflicts and struggles that ensued gave a life and vitality to eighteenth-century politics which steadily engulfed larger sections of the population. Political life in the eighteenth century was therefore always richer, freer, more open than the oligarchical nature of its institutions might lead one to believe. And this gave Englishmen in this century a political experience that was unique. The richness and variety of that experience has received recently all too little attention. As far as the eighteenth century is concerned, political decisions and the turmoil they aroused are the heart of politics, not elections. It is time we returned to their study.

CHAPTER 2

MAN'S ECONOMIC STATUS

by Jacob Viner

I have found myself struggling somewhat with the assigned title of my paper. To give me some finite bodies of matter to focus on, I will concentrate on restricted categories of 'man', of 'society', and of material that can justify the 'economic' label. Since neither 1701 nor 1801 have appreciable terminal significance for any problem or issue within my range of knowledge, 1688, the year of the Glorious Revolution, will be my approximate beginning date, and the period after 1776 will be referred to only now and again, not because this later period is unimportant or uninteresting to me, but on the contrary because it differs enough for my purposes from the period that preceded it to justify its being segregated for separate treatment. 'Britain' I will take to mean England. Scotland even after the Union remained largely another country, different substantially in its social thought, its legal system, its political and economic structure, its educational and religious institutions and principles. Ireland was a colony of a peculiar kind, even more distinguishable from England in many respects relevant for my lecture than were Scotland and the American Colonies. If 'versus' means opposed to, I will spend more time on 'Society versus Man' than on 'Man versus Society', and will even pause to ask 'What is Man?' and attempt a reply in terms of different social categories of man as he was in eighteenth-century England. Aside from these particulars, I will conform strictly to the assigned title of my lecture.

'Man versus Society' or 'Man versus the State' would have served me very well as the title for a lecture on *laissez faire* or on 'economic individualism', in eighteenth-century England, were I not at a loss for supporting data of historical significance prior to the publication, in 1776, of Adam Smith's *Wealth of Nations*. Even Adam Smith did not succeed in making *laissez faire* a live issue for discussion and agitation until the turn of the century, and I am not enough of an economic historian to detect a clear trend in the actual course of events in these respects in either direction as between 'freedom' and 'social control' before the beginning of the nineteenth century. There was of course much talk of 'freedom' or of 'liberty' before and throughout the eighteenth century, but it was not often in the sense of any modern abstract term of wide meaning. Even when the talk was of 'liberty' in the singular as far as phrasing went, it was often of 'liberties' in the plural or of a very specific type of liberty as far as meaning went. It was often quite clear that what its possessor called a liberty was by those who did not possess it but would have liked to enjoy it regarded as a special privilege, and by those who wished no one to possess it was looked on as licence. Abstract terms in '-ism' were not yet current outside the field of theology and indeed I can think of only one instance of the use of an '-ism' term in the period in a work of economic relevance. This was in the title of a 1713 anonymous tract, *Torism and Trade Can Never Agree*, a title whose translation into twentieth-century English would call for some fairly detailed acquaintance with the political issues of that year. In the interest of keeping as close as is practicable to my eighteenth-century sources, I have tried, I believe successfully, to resist the temptation to use in this lecture any '-ism' terminology.

In the England of my period, the miracle was performed of simultaneous tight regulation of foreign trade, wide-ranging though somewhat haphazard intervention by government in domestic economic matters, and limitations of government personnel to a minuscule national and local bureaucracy and government-employed work force except in the field of tax collection. Even such activities as police, fire protection, the conduct of the Mint, the postal service, the construction and maintenance of roads, canals, harbours, lighthouses, education, the provisioning of the army, the operation of jails, the servicing and accounting of the national debt, street-cleaning, garbage disposal, water supply, street-lighting, regulation of domestic industry and trade were in large part or in entirety farmed out or abandoned to private-profit enterprise, to individual charitable initiative, or to the ancient guilds. The government of British India was entrusted to a chartered company operating for profit.

This was in a sense a manifestation of 'man versus the state', of citizenry limiting the scope of direct activity of government. It was especially a manifestation of mistrust by the ruling sector of the public of the English central government as it had operated in the past and, if permitted, would probably operate in the future. There was jealousy of executive power, as contrasted with parliamentary power or with power of the judiciary. Parliament could not itself undertake administrative tasks involving large numbers of employees. Entrusting the executive with such tasks meant entrusting it with large payrolls, which could be used to buy political support, to make placemen out of members of parliament and members of parliament out of placemen, to reward political service rendered to the executive by members of either House and by anyone else. To strengthen the executive meant to strengthen the role of the Crown as against that of the nobility and the gentry. To avoid this, parliament held the executive to a total bureaucratic force other than military personnel and tax officials of, at the end of the century, barely 2,000 men for the entire central government, inclusive of holders of sinecure posts. This combination of intervention through legislation with only a skeleton of bureaucracy to operate the system has in modern times been labelled 'administrative nihilism'. It could be labelled 'indirect government', or 'government with a minimum of bureaucracy'.[1]

Mistrust of the central government was associated with mistrust of and dislike of the direct exercise of power by its officers. It was not opposition to government on principle. The mistrust did not extend, moreover, to the magistrates, to whom fell many tasks which in other countries were performed by administrative personnel. The agent of the central government whom an ordinary citizen of middle rank was most likely to encounter would be a collector of excise or of customs. A member of the lower classes in a seaport might encounter also a press-gang endeavouring to seize him for service in the Navy. No national government employees were to be seen building roads or canals or water-supply systems, or teaching, or providing police or sanitation services, or giving weather-reporting services to the public. I do not suppose that there is now or ever was particular affection in any country for customs and tax collectors. If it was with these categories of central officialdom that citizens would mainly have contact, mistrust of government and mistrust and dislike of its agents would reinforce each other. Contact with government in action would readily be felt to involve or threaten an invasion of the privacy of the individual by an agency, the state, foreign to him and hostile to him.

In 1733 the Robert Walpole administration was forced by a nation-wide outburst of protest to withdraw its bill to substitute excise duties on tobacco and wines collected internally at the warehouses of the merchants for the existing customs duties collected at the ports at the time of landing and the associated drawbacks of tax upon such portions of the imports as were re-exported to foreign countries. It was the objective of the bill to provide a remedy for the wholesale frauds associated with both the collection of the import duties and the payment of drawbacks, and involving, the government claimed, serious loss of revenue. The proposal, however, would have required an expansion of the hated corps of excisemen, the inquisitorial visitation of tradesmen's premises, and, according to the opposition, an escape by the executive of dependence on annual vote by parliament with respect to the expenditure of the revenue derived from the proposed excise taxes. The opposition also aroused the public to interpret the proposal as only the first step in an insidious programme to expand indefinitely the scope of the excise tax system, and harped on the fact that persons charged with violations of tax laws faced more arbitrary administrative and legal hazards if the taxes were excises than if they were import duties. It was this last point which Samuel Johnson had in mind when in his *Dictionary* he defined 'excise' as 'a hateful tax levied upon commodities and adjudged not by the common judges of property [that is, the magistrates] but by wretches [i.e. excisemen] hired by those to whom the excise is paid'.[1]

In 1763, public dislike of an excise measure was again to shake the government. In that year the administration, under the leadership of the earl of Bute, had carried through parliament, against strong opposition, an excise tax on cider, probably a more important commodity at the time as an adulterant of wine and thus a means of escape from customs duties on imported wine than as a beverage on its own account. The cider tax authorised entrance by excise officers into homes, to search for and collect tax on home-brewed cider. The old cry was raised that 'an Englishman's house was his castle', although only for the country gentlemen and the substantial farmers was it practicable to make their homes serve also as untaxed cider-mills. But an encroachment on *their* privacy was not a politically viable step. The outcry against the tax forced Bute to resign from office, and the succeeding Rockingham ministry in 1765 repealed the tax.[2]

The preamble of one of the first acts of William and Mary's reign abrogating a hearth-money tax introduced in Charles I's reign explained that the tax was 'not only a great oppression upon the poorer sort, but a badge of slavery upon the whole people; exposing every man's house to be entered into, and searched at pleasure, by persons unknown to him'.[3] A proposal in 1756 in the House of Commons for authorisation of the government to take a census of the number of the people was defeated after a member of the House had attacked the proposal as, among other things, involving an invasion of the people's privacy. 'I did not believe', he exclaimed, 'that there had been any set of men, or indeed, any individual of the human species, so presumptuous and so abandoned, as to make the proposal which we have just heard.'[1] Adam Smith, in *The Wealth of Nations*, condemned income taxes as necessarily involving an unacceptable encroachment on privacy. 'The state of a man's fortune varies from day to day, and without an inquisition more intolerable than any tax, and renewed at least once a year, can only be guessed at.'[2]

What means did the Englishman have of coping with a State he regarded as oppressive or offensive? After 1688, the landowners were in effect the State, through parliament, as long as they kept a bridle on the king and his ministers. Much of the political history of the eighteenth century revolved around the relations of the substantial landowners with the Crown and among themselves in the processes of winning elections, managing parliament, and conducting local political affairs. These landowners were most of the time well able to protect themselves against oppression by the 'State', and there was no other power in a position to oppress or coerce them.

From here on, I will abandon my concern for the landed gentry, and will concentrate on the 'labouring poor', urban and rural, some living on self-employment, but most of them dependent on wages, on public and private charity, or on unrespectable or 'invisible' means of support. The really poor portion of the 'poor' I take to have comprised, with their dependants, at a minimum somewhere between 50 per cent at the beginning and 40 per cent at the end of the century. In this 40–50 per cent would be included, as far as wage labour is concerned, the great bulk of those of whom Adam Smith said: 'Many workmen could not subsist a week, few could subsist a month, and scarce any a year without employment.'[3]

I should warn you, however, that whatever gestures toward

quantification I make in this lecture rest mostly on contemporary conjectures. Official statistics were either not gathered or had gross error systematically built into them. Modern presentations of what purport to be statistics of or for the eighteenth century either do not cover the aspects I am concerned with in this lecture, or are too fragmentary or too much the product of promiscuous aggregation to be trusted as representative, or are conjectures expressed in numerical form which owe more to the imagination of their authors than to supporting evidence. Fully as I respect the current zeal for expert quantification of history as a virtue in itself, I regard it, like all other virtues, as competitive with other values, such as, in the present instances, relevance to fact and relevance to questions that non-statisticians care to ask. In this instance, as in many others, I find the judgment or even conjecture of a *contemporary* person of presumptive honesty and intelligence often the safest guide available, though rarely a safe guide. It is prudent always to bear in mind that detailed bits of evidence constitute the sole genuine records of high or even moderate reliability that the past bequeaths to us. In any case, from now on my concern will be with a lower segment of the population, substantial in size, constituting those of the urban and rural 'labouring poor' who were poor by inheritance and class status. The poor by accident, the members of families with a tradition of at least moderate prosperity who by misfortune or misconduct had fallen into poverty, were commonly excluded from the category of 'labouring poor'. Of the thinking and the experience of genuine members of the labouring poor we have almost no authentic record. Our knowledge of their feelings and hopes, of their pleasures and pains, of the conditions of their day-to-day life, is based almost completely on the reports of observers, often with personal or ideological axes to grind, and not on the testimony of the poor themselves. Any modern history of 'English thought' in the eighteenth century, we should remember, is almost certain to be solely or mainly, at its most comprehensive, a history of the expressed thought of the upper-half English.

In the vocabulary of the upper half the lower half was often not included, or included in a very qualified sense, in the denotation of the word 'people'. According to Edmund Burke, the natural strength of the kingdom, identified with the 'people', consisted of 'the great peers, the leading landed gentlemen, the opulent merchants and manufacturers, the substantial yeomanry'.[1] A Whig preacher, John Brown, in 1765 defined the 'people' in similar terms: 'the landed gentry, the beneficed country clergy, many of the more considerable merchants and men in trade, the substantial and industrious freeholders or yeomen.'[2] At about the same time, the *Political Register* attacked the problem of definition of 'people' from the other end, specifying those who were to be excluded from the term: 'the illiterate rabble, who have neither capacity for judging of matters of government, nor property to be concerned for.'[3] For the excluded there was no shortage of labels: they were the 'poor', the 'populace', the 'rabble', the 'mob', the 'scum'. To William Petty, they were the 'poor people', constituting, whether wholly or mostly he does not make explicit, 'the vile and brutish part of mankind'.[4] Sometimes they were referred to as 'mere people', as distinguished from those above them in social status and thus more than 'mere'.

It is amusing that in France verbal usage was sometimes the reverse of this: only those who had to resort to physical labour for their living were designated as 'le peuple'. Voltaire especially followed this usage: 'By people I mean the populace that only has its hands to work with. I doubt whether that class of citizens will ever have time or capacity for education.' 'France would be a delightful country if it were not for its taxes and its pedants. As to the people, they will always be stupid and barbarous. They are cattle and what is wanted for them is a yoke, a goad, and fodder.'[5]

The English labouring poor were in England almost completely without the semblance of recognised political power. As employees they could sometimes manage to organise, illegally but with occasional effectiveness, into sketchy anticipations of modern labour unions and strike against or otherwise harass their employers. As individuals they could rebel against their low status in the social order by abandoning steady work and resorting to vagabondage or begging or petty thievery. If sufficiently provoked by events, they could, and frequently did, resort to riot. But only exceptionally did any of them have voting rights of any kind.

The upper classes did not take riots lightly. They attributed to riots a contagious quality, and they were conscious that they could be generated by a wide range of factors which to them were cherished features of the English social structure. Of modern types of police there was scarcely a trace, and once order was disturbed an amateur militia or regular military forces had to be called in on an emergency basis to restore quiet. Benjamin Franklin wrote on the margin of an English pamphlet of 1769: 'I have seen, within a year, riots in the country about corn; riots about elections; riots about workhouses; riots of colliers; riots of weavers; riots of coal-heavers; riots of sawyers; riots of Wilkesites; riots of government [licensed?] chairmen; riots of smugglers, in which custom-house officers and excisemen have been murdered, [and] the King's armed vessels and troops fired at.'[1] In other years he could have seen or read about other occasions for riots, riots against Catholics, of cottagers against enclosures, of farm-labourers against labour-saving machinery, and so on.

Many members of the upper classes were suspicious of the consequences of literacy on the part of the working classes, and many of the working class were illiterate, in fact a majority of them if the ability to write is taken as the test of 'literacy'. It may be, however, that from the point of view of peace and order there can be either too much literacy or too little, and that literacy restricted to a few of the lower classes is the most dangerous state of all, since a demogogic literate few could capture the minds of the illiterate many by reading to or speaking to them. A Swiss visitor to England reported in 1726, no doubt with at least a trace of exaggeration: 'All Englishmen are great newsmongers. Workmen habitually begin the day by going to coffee-rooms in order to read the latest news. I have often seen shoeblacks and other persons of that class club together to purchase a farthing paper. Nothing is more entertaining than hearing men of this class discussing politics and topics of interest concerning royalty.'[1] An upper-class Englishman might, perhaps, have found the discussion, if he had overheard it, more terrifying than entertaining.

I must now take awkward leave of 'Man versus Society' and the State to turn to society and the State versus the labouring man. There was of course in the class structure of eighteenth-century England a continuous gradation stretching from the dizzy heights of royalty and nobility down to the lowest depths of miserable and hungry and degraded creatures, a gradation known to the theologians and poets of the period as part of that admirable creation of God, the 'great chain of being'. Limitations of time and of knowledge force me to lump together as one group something like half of the links in the human part of the chain, the lower half, the poverty-in-the-midst-of-plenty half. The lack of data as to the thought of this lower half about their own social condition forces me also to confine myself to the thought of the upper half relating to the other half.

Much of English eighteenth-century upper-class thought about the phenomenon of poverty was of course not peculiar to England or to that century. Influences from the ancient classics, from serviceable elements of the Christian moral tradition, from the Continental Enlightenment, can easily be identified. But the special character of English conditions and traditions and the capacity of the English mind for original or idiosyncratic thought did lead to some differences between English ideas with respect to poverty and the ideas prevalent in other countries. Anglicanism, the role in society of the country gentleman, content with the

'Matchless Constitution', the administratively inert and inept government, the pervasive dislike of 'enthusiasm' in all fields, were, in degree and to some extent in kind, aspects of society peculiar to England and operating to give its prevalent doctrines about poverty a distinctive English flavour. There was much that was distinctively English in the English ideas about poverty, and much of what was written in England at the time relating to poverty sounded foreign to foreigners and even to Scotsmen. One institution peculiar to England when on a national scale was what was known on the Continent as 'legal charity' or the acceptance by government of legal obligations to relieve on a systematic basis economic distress, the cost to be defrayed by compulsory levies on the propertied classes. I will have occasion later to deal in some detail with this once peculiarly English institution, now of course a nearly universal phenomenon. It gave a special character to all English utterances on voluntary charity, since only in England was there to a significant degree any other kind of charity.

The English Anglican charity sermons provide an invaluable guide to upper-class English thought with respect to the poor. An Anglican clergyman of high status would be a representative member of the upper classes. The charity sermon was periodically addressed to the upper classes at prayer and had as its primary function to persuade the prosperous to continue and, in moderation, to improve on their past record of contributions to charitable purposes. To be successful in achieving its purpose, the charity sermon had to avoid challenging the social philosophy of its audience. To be honest, and to appear so to its audience, the sermon also had to reflect the social philosophy of the preacher. The charity sermons of the great French preachers that I have read were in these respects radically different. The condition of the French poor was probably more desperate than that of the English. Charity in France was not merely a supplement to regularly established and comprehensive legal or official relief, but was the only source of help for the distressed. The issue of life and death of many persons depended on the response made to pleas for charity by the French preachers. The urgency of voluntary giving was therefore greater than in England. The Catholic preacher had less doctrinal sanction for lax preaching. He was also less subject than was an Anglican dignitary to social pressure or pressure from important parishioners to maintain harmony between his utterances and the attitudes of his audience. In consequence, a Bourdaloue, a Massillon, could without hesitation address his most aristocratic audiences as sinners whose salvation was specially in jeopardy and who urgently needed to practice generous and even heroic charity as an afterlife insurance policy.[1]

An English charity sermon was, in contrast, while insistent on the duty of giving, typically abounding in reservations and limitations as to the extent of giving which was religiously or morally obligatory or socially beneficial.[2] It frequently included expressions of deference to the establishment comfortably seated in the pews and of admonitions specially addressed to the poor standing in the aisles or at the rear concerning their obligations to be industrious, to be frugal, to be humble and respectful to their betters, to be patient in enduring hardship, and to be grateful for benefits received.

Another Anglican eighteenth-century institution was the charity school, on behalf of which special sermons were given annually in London in solicitation of voluntary gifts to support the schools.[3] These charity school sermons were also customary in Ireland, where the charity schools, however, were largely boarding, not day schools, and had as one of their primary objectives the conversion of poor Catholic children to protestantism by drawing them away from their home surroundings. There was in England no publicly financed education to compete with the charity schools. The upper-class judgment as to how much education it was good for the poor, good for the country, and good for the rich that the children of the poor should receive rarely rose above a very elementary level of reading, writing, and arithmetic, and often insisted that the ability to write was a luxury for the children of the rural poor and liable to undermine their willingness to conform to the status providentially assigned to them in the rural pattern of life. Teaching of writing was in many rural charity schools deliberately omitted, lest, in the words of a charity school sermon of 1743 by Bishop Thomas Secker, it 'possibly may turn the minds of children, or of their parents for them, to some other business than husbandry'.[1]

Bernard Mandeville in his *Fable of the Bees* attacked the charity schools on the ground that they were overeducating the children and thus making them unfit for their appropriate function in society, which was to be docile hewers of wood and drawers of water in the service of the national economy.[2] Infidel though he may have been, there is no doubt that on this issue there were many of the faithful who agreed with him, and charity school sermons often included denials of his charge that the charity schools had these effects on the children. While the sponsors of the charity schools, on grounds of humanity and religion, defended provision of a bare literacy for even the lowest strata of the social structure, they insisted that the teaching was, or should be, carefully kept to a very elementary level, and that religious and moral disciplinary training, suitable to the status in life that the children were providentially destined for, was the primary objective of the schools.[3] The attendance at the schools reached a peak of 60,000 for all of England. Their financing never was easy, and the charity school movement petered out before the end of the century, to be replaced after an interval by the Sunday school, a cheaper substitute, since, as it operated only one day a week, it needed no fulltime or professional staff, and did not compete for the time of the children with the workshop or the farm.

I know only of Bishops Butler, Stillingfleet and Shipley and of a few dissenters who in eighteenth-century England explicitly urged a more generous level of education for the children of the poor both on outright religious and humanitarian grounds and to increase upward social mobility.

Shipley delivered in 1777 a charity school sermon which is noteworthy for its explicit and sharp disavowal of the aristocratic bias and the excessive preaching of other-worldliness to the poor in the literature distributed by the charity school movement, including presumably the series of previously published charity school sermons, and for its criticism of the insistence in this literature that 'the sole intention of our religion is to prepare its followers for a better life [i.e. in another world], without any immediate regard to their happiness at present'. 'Prudence in the conduct of life', he claimed, 'is a superior and a master virtue, and should not be debased to superficial and trifling austerities.' It was 'the intention of our creator...that all men should concur in procuring that happiness which every man wishes for, and which every man has an equal capacity to acquire and an equal right to expect'.[1]

It was repeatedly claimed in the eighteenth century on behalf of England that 'equality before the law' prevailed there. I know of no grounds for disputing that this claim came closer to realisation in fact in England, and also in Scotland, than in any other important country or region of the world. But the term 'equality before the law' has its due measure of ambiguity.

Richard Savage was a poet, and, although we may regard as somewhat of an exaggeration David Hume's comment that poets are 'liars by profession', I doubt whether anyone in the eighteenth century would have challenged seriously Dryden's statement that it is proper for a poet, when doing honour to his country, to exaggerate its merits somewhat, 'for he is not tied to truth, or fettered by the laws of history'. Savage, therefore, was staying within the customary limits of poetic licence when he claimed on behalf of England:

> Who digs the mine or quarry, digs with glee;
> No slave—His option and his gain are free:
> Him the same laws the same protection yield,
> Who plows the furrow, as who owns the field.[2]

Another poet, James Thomson, freely exercising his poetic licence to pay tribute to 'Liberty' as it prevailed in Britain, dwelt for a moment on what it meant for the poor:

> For Toil, by thee protected, feels no pain,
> The poor man's lot with milk and honey flows,
> And, gilded with thy rays, even death looks gay.[1]

We think of the principle of 'equality before the law' as meaning that all persons who come before the law do so on a basis 'equal' in all relevant respects. The most ardent exponent of equality before the law might hesitate, however, before supporting literally identical treatment of men and women, adults and children, the strong and the weak, the responsible and the idiots. There is in fact much in modern law which is widely approved because it deliberately deals more gently with the weak than with the strong.

There were undoubtedly instances in which the impact of English eighteenth-century law was administratively tempered to the shorn lamb, but I have been able to find only one instance of a statute imposing penalties for misconduct where the penalties were graded upward according to the social status of the offender. This was the Profane Oaths Act of 1746, which laid penalties for swearing of one shilling for a day-labourer, common soldier or common seaman, of two shillings for everybody else under the degree of a gentleman, and of five shillings for gentlemen and upwards, including presumably royalty.[2]

Whatever the intent of the framers of legislation, from the time at least of ancient Greece it has been a commonplace, and perhaps therefore true, that, in the words attributed to Anacharsis, 'Laws are merely spider webs, which the birds, being larger, break through with ease, while the flies are caught fast'. In eighteenth-century English law, in any case, the birds and the flies were often not treated alike, and the distinctions made between them by common law, by statutory law, and in the administration of the law, often deliberately and explicitly favoured the birds.

Such was the opinion of Samuel Johnson. 'No scheme of policy', he wrote, 'has, in any country, yet brought the rich and poor on equal terms into courts of judicature. Perhaps experience, improving on experience, may in time effect it.'[1] In Henry Fielding's *Joseph Andrews*, Lady Booby consults the unscrupulous lawyer, Scout, as to the possibility of using the settlement laws to prevent her servant, Joseph Andrews, on whom she had unchaste designs of her own, from marrying his beloved Fanny within the parish. The lawyer replies: 'The laws of this land are not so vulgar to permit a mean fellow [like Andrews] to contend with one of your ladyship's fortune.'[2] Richard Parrott, writing in 1752, criticised the ways in which the laws relating to morals were drawn, leaving the gentlemen exempt. He commented that it was not ordinarily within the power of the magistrates as such to remedy this, but that Henry Fielding, as both a magistrate and a novelist with great influence on the upper classes, was an exception: 'this admired writer has now the sole means of authority over gentlemen, which perhaps no other magistrate in the world ever had; for he is the first who ever joined propriety in active life as a civil officer, with acknowledged superiority as a man of genius.'[3]

The ferociousness, judged by prevailing present-day standards, of English eighteenth-century criminal law is well known. It was not an eighteenth-century innovation, however, and it was probably exceeded in some other countries. There were eighteenth-century ameliorations, moreover, such as greater resort to the pardoning power, and the refusal of juries to convict because of the severity of the penalties, which operated to make the application of the criminal law less harsh than the letter of the statutes. Modern experts offer different explanations of the revolution in the direction of mildness which occurred in criminal law after the eighteenth century. Much emphasis is put on the defects in the eighteenth-century techniques of prevention and detection of crime and of apprehension of criminals, with the consequence that the respectable classes had great fear of the criminal class and, given the high probability of escape from punishment of any particular offender, were convinced that very severe penalties for those who were caught and convicted were essential if the laws were to have much deterrent effect.

I am here concerned only with the extent to which, in the area of economic offences, the scale of penalties was class structured so as to fall with disproportionate severity on violators of property rights of a kind with which the rich were specially, and even exclusively, concerned, or to fall with disproportionate severity on offences of which the lowest classes were likely to be preponderant or even exclusive perpetrators.

My chief impression in this connection is that so general a lack of apparent system and logic in the criminal law was operative in the eighteenth century that to attribute system and consistency to its biases is, from the point of view of efficiency in government, unduly generous. The criminal law was the product of a disorderly sequence of piecemeal enactments stretching over centuries, unplanned, uncodified, never methodically evaluated as a whole, and administered with an almost total lack of order and expertise. As a part of the established legal structure of England, entitled as such to respect and even veneration, it was regarded as not properly subject to critical examination, whether for violations of humanity or for inefficiency as instruments of deterrence of crime, or for other kinds of defect. Depending on who does the counting, there were in the eighteenth century from 150 to 250 capital offences, that is crimes for which death was the minimum penalty. By 1850, there were only two. Now, I believe, there is only one, or is it none? Although comparative numbers like these are still repeatedly cited as evidence of the harshness of eighteenth-century penal law, they can be somewhat misleading. As Justice J. F. Stephen, in 1883, pointed out, a single act making larceny in general punishable by death would be more severe than fifty separate acts making fifty specific varieties of larceny so punishable, if there remained some species of larceny not covered by these acts.[1] But we need not worry too much about this fine point, if in the next century *no* species of larceny bore the death penalty. It was, moreover, the apparent lack of rationality as well as the severity of eighteenth-century criminal law which was later to bring about its comprehensive reform. Among the offences subject to the death penalty in the eighteenth century were: stealing from a boat on a navigable river, but not on a canal; stealing from the person to the value of one shilling, from a shop to the value of five shillings, and from a dwelling-house to the value of forty shillings; entering land with intent to kill game or rabbits. Murderous assault, however, was not a capital offence if the victim survived the attack.[2] Data such as these make it entirely plausible that particular penalties manifest clear-cut class bias, but they warn against imputing to the system as a whole any consistent pattern of bias, or any other understandable rationale.

Particular instances of outstanding bias can easily be cited, however, as showing what the century was capable of tolerating. The game laws provide a unique example where it was encroachments on exclusive privileges artificially established by law for the very rich that were capital offences. The trapping or shooting of game was an exclusive privilege of the large landowners. Small landowners and tenants of any scale were not allowed to trap or shoot game on even the land which they owned or occupied. The only justification offered in an eighteenth-century law guide for this aspect of the game laws was that these laws were enacted 'for the recreation and amusement of persons of fortune...and to prevent persons of inferior rank from squandering that time which their station of life requireth to be profitably employed'.[3] Perhaps, however, the enactors of this legislation had better reasons for it than I have found recorded. Since private efforts to preserve game can be practicable only if they apply to extensive areas of land, only large-scale proprietors would have a definite personal gain from preserving game rather than shooting it as fast as they could. To give exclusive shooting privileges to great proprietors on their neighbour's as well as on their own land and on their own land even when it was occupied by rent-paying tenants may have been the most effective game preservative available. But capital punishment for illegal shooting still seems harsh, especially if, as was notoriously a common situation, game birds in their depredations on the growing crops made no exemptions in favour of the crops of small landowners, tenants, and cottagers with a few acres of grain.

The 'benefit of clergy' clause in criminal legislation applying to many types of offences was in effect an indisputable though increasingly imprecise distinction between persons according to their social status. In its twelfth-century origins this phrase signified the right of clergy to be tried for offences in ecclesiastical instead of in civil courts, and it is conceivable that canon law was often more severe than civil law. At that period, few but the clergy were literate. By a centuries-long process the clause evolved into a pattern of substitution for literate offenders, whether they were clerics or not, of other penalties than death if they pleaded benefit of clergy. The eighteenth century inherited this discriminatory practice, but long before the century was over allowed it to obsolesce.[1]

Tampering with the coinage for private profit was from ancient times severely punished because of the conviction that it caused damage to the working of a vital community service and involved the equivalent of stealing of public property. In the early 1690s England was undergoing a major monetary crisis as a consequence of the deterioration of the coinage resulting in part from coin-clipping and other methods of abstracting metal from the coins before passing them on as legal tender. Some years before, capital punishment had been decreed for this offence in substitution for older penalties involving several degrees of mutilation and torture. William Fleetwood, chaplain to the king and later bishop of Ely, in 1694 delivered a sermon against clipping. Fleetwood was one of the many clergymen who compounded his theology with economics and vice versa. Lord Keynes, in 1941, in a letter to Archbishop Temple encouraging him to continue to speak with assurance in public discussion of economic issues, cited Fleetwood as one of a sizeable group of clergymen who in his century were almost alone in developing politico-economic thought.[1] In his sermon Fleetwood expressed regret for the substitution for the penalties imposed for coin-clipping in older times of what he regarded as the unduly mild punishment of death. His sermon is the clearest contemporary expression I have found of the type of reasoning which could then lead men of the most estimable character to accept and approve penalties of the most extreme harshness for what they regarded as major crimes against a country's economic institutions. Here are two relevant passages from his sermon:

The laws of our country in King Athelstan's time, punished them... with the cutting off their right-hand, and fixing them [i.e. their hands] over the place where they committed the offence. In King Ethelred's days they were to undergo the *treble ordeal*, i.e., to carry a red-hot iron of three pound weight in their hands such a determined space of ground, and if they miscarried there, they were to die. In Henry I's time they were condemned to lose, some their hands, and some their eyes... These punishments were after chang'd into the modern executions, and have so continued ever since, altho 'tis probable that punishments of greater pain and constant shame, such as they heretofore were, would secure us better than putting many to a short and easy death...

And if there appears but little of Christianity in such sermons [as this one], it will be to such as consider not, how great a part justice and honesty, and fair and righteous dealing, make up of this divine religion, and how great care the doctrines of the Gospel take, not only of men's souls in the world to come, but of the good and welfare of their bodies here.[2]

Imprisonment for debt is the only category of legislation of economic relevance that I have found which from the seventeenth to the nineteenth century gave rise to a continuing and impressive series of protests resting, in part at least, on strictly humanitarian grounds. This series of protests was left substantially unanswered, but some minor changes in the laws in the direction of lesser harshness were made before the end of the eighteenth century.

Humanitarian objection to imprisonment for debt arose from a sense of inappropriateness in degree of the punishment to the offence. It arose also from the failure of the legislation to differentiate between those who were fraudulently delinquent and those who were innocent victims of misfortune. The fact that the jails were managed as private enterprises by licensed jailers operating for private profit and subject to no obligations to feed the prisoners or to maintain prescribed standards of sanitary and other facilities was also subjected to vigorous criticism. The jailers in fact operated what could be called delinquent-debtor hotels, and they depended for their compensation on what they could extort from the inmates or their outside friends for food, quarters, and facilities. Deliquency in debt, it may be important to notice, could happen to members of any social class, and a record of those imprisoned for debt and of their close relatives would include an astounding number of names of authors, artists, poets, clergymen, and others who later attained some degree of eminence. Samuel Johnson, who made some of the most sensible and most constructive criticisms of the laws against debtors published during the century, reported estimates, for a period when the population of England did not exceed 6,000,000, that at any one time 20,000 would be in prison because of debt, of whom about one-fourth would die each year from the hardships of prison life.[1]

What explanation can be offered for this survival of a practice which in its own time had many critics and few open defenders? The practice did not clearly serve the self-interest of any substantial social group except those creditors who were convinced that the delinquency of debtors was largely wilful and fraudulent or that the indefinite imprisonment of even innocent debtors would coerce their families or friends into liquidating their indebtedness. As in most other areas, legislative ingenuity and good public administration were here woefully lacking, and there had been no real attempt to find procedures whereby the fraudulent debtor could be penalised without treating the innocent debtor in identical manner. There was in the middle and especially the commercial classes a strong feeling that, even without any fraudulent intent, it was sinful to get into debt beyond one's certain ability to repay on schedule. There was among them, as well as among members of other social groups, the belief that the punctual meeting of financial engagements was so vital, so sacred, a part of the code of civilised society, that no considerations of humanity should be permitted to weaken the sanctions which society imposed on those who did not fulfil to the letter the requirements of that code.[1] Harshness of treatment of violators of accepted moral principles, in this as in other fields, was often defended by the theological principle that the obligation of mercy was not applicable for offenders if it involved, directly or indirectly, withholding mercy from their innocent victims, actual or potential. It was a defect of the proposers of reform on humanitarian grounds that they did not adequately apply themselves to formulating alternative procedures which would give promise of preserving and even strengthening pressure for performance of contract without resort to the practice of imprisonment for debt. Progress in this was not to be achieved until the next century.

The English poor laws came close to being a purely English institution without a parallel on a national scale anywhere on the Continent, or, for that matter, in Scotland or Ireland. They required each parish to provide relief in cash or kind to those poor with right of settlement in that parish, and to finance the relief by local 'rates' or taxes based on the rental value of landed property. The poor laws were a post-Reformation institution, and were introduced as a substitute for the alms distributed by the Catholic Church from its landed and other endowments and from the current flow of donations to it by the faithful. The English system was later to be pejoratively labelled 'legal charity' by continental Catholics, and to be characterised by them as morally inferior to a system, consisting exclusively of voluntary individual charity and of more-or-less organised charity administered by the Church, which did not establish legal rights on the part of the beneficiaries or legal obligations on the part of the donors. In Scotland, relief to the poor made obligatory by law was almost universally opposed as presenting obstacles to discrimination between deserving and undeserving poor, and, by making relief in case of distress a safe expectation, undermining the natural incentives for the poor to practice industry, frugality, and other economic virtues. Scottish commentators, with scarcely any exception that I have been able to find before 1840, were uniformly critical of the English system. They found especially objectionable in the English system the necessity of protecting the property owners in the individual parishes from the hazard of unlimited tax burdens by associating, with the obligation on each parish to grant relief to those in need and having legal rights of settlement within that parish, the imposition of an elaborate and harsh code of discipline on even the most industrious and well-behaved of the labouring classes. This code restricted their right of migration from parish to parish, authorised the taking away of young children from the custody of their parents if the latter were on relief, interfered with rights of marriage, and in many other ways abridged basic freedoms of the lower classes. Those who sought escape from the poor-law discipline by resorting to vagrancy or 'going on the road' were subjected to penalties so brutal that a thoroughly unsentimental English authority on the poor laws, Richard Burn, could write in 1764 that 'This part of our history looks like the history of the savages in America. Almost all severities have been exercised against vagrants, except scalping.'[1]

There was little enthusiasm in England itself for the poor laws, and they were supported mostly as partial remedies for evils for which less objectionable remedies were not in sight. In some quarters there was radical opposition to them on principle or because of their unsatisfactory mode of operation. They were of such long standing, however, so deeply entangled with the English wage structure, labour-hiring methods, and lower-class patterns of family formation, that anything more than piecemeal and gradual change would have been a revolutionary step. Major poor-law reform had to wait until the nineteenth century, although throughout the eighteenth century there was a steady flow of suggestions for change in the poor-laws.

Some of these proposals for change were for more generous treatment of the 'deserving poor', the involuntarily unemployed and the physically handicapped, but almost all of them recommended more severe treatment of the 'undeserving poor'. Some of the proposals advised that the territorial units for assessment of poor rates and for defining the boundaries for legal settlement be extended to include more than a single parish. An ever-present objective was the economic one of making the poor a more productive resource for the national economy, by reducing the number who were voluntarily or involuntarily idle. There were schemes galore for making the poorest of the poor self-supporting by gathering them in workhouses and putting them to work under official supervision, the aged, the young children, the physically or mentally handicapped, the wilfully idle, included. Even without consideration of the desperately low standards, national and local, of public administration in England in the century most of these schemes were visionary in character in their assumption that ways could be found of immediately making the least eligible sections of the population not only self-supporting but producers of a net contribution to the national economy.

The most visionary of such schemes was, if I interpret it correctly, a proposal made by Bishop Berkeley in 1721 that there be raised by act of parliament annually for seven years an amount equal to the average annual yield of the poor rates, the proceeds to be expended on workhouses.[1] Berkeley promised that if prudently managed this 'would for ever free the nation from the care of providing for the poor, and at the same time considerably improve our manufactures. We might by these means rid our streets of beggars; even the children, the maimed, and the blind might be put in a way of doing something for their livelihood.'[1]

In anything like an exhaustive treatment of ideas and practices in eighteenth-century England relating to advocacy of or hostility or indifference to what later generations regarded as 'social reform' I would have to deal extensively with the general field of taxation and at least to mention so peculiarly English a phenomenon as the press-gang as a method of recruiting for the navy, as well as other matters, some of which I am no doubt unaware of. One generalisation I am, however, willing to commit myself to: the politically important sectors of the English population were not *laissez faire* on principle, and accepted as a matter of course a substantial measure of state intervention, provided it used techniques of administration tolerable to them and provided government did not tamper with the prevailing social structure. A present-day eighteenth-century scholar of distinction, Thomas W. Copeland, has heralded as 'probably the most important single act of reform achieved in England in the eighteenth century' the Economical Reform Act of 1780, sponsored by Edmund Burke.[2] The Act was in fact of minor scope and of debated and debatable effectiveness, but I nevertheless cannot challenge this appraisal of it. The American and the French Revolutions did serve to widen and deepen the range of political and economic discussion, and to introduce change into the air, although little of this change manifested itself on the ground until after the turn of the century. Of major importance, conducive in a host of subtle ways to social change, was the growth in size of the middle classes relative to the gentry and to the proletariat, but the effects of this growth are in the main not easy to perceive until well after 1800. The French Revolution, in fact, by the fear it engendered in the upper classes of like threat to their own vested interests in England, stimulated reaction rather than either strategic reform or mere continuance of the previously prevailing complacent, moderate, and stagnant conservatism of which Edmund Burke had been the most eloquent exponent.

More significant, I think, than the Economical Reform Act of 1780 as a harbinger of things to come in another generation or two was the astonishing speed with which John Howard, by a one-man effort, persuaded parliament to enact in 1774 a measure of genuine prison reform, requiring government and its agents to accept financial and supervisory responsibility for the payment of jailers, the cleaning of prisons, and the decent care of prisoners. English prisons had been notorious for the unregulated authority their jailers wielded, and for the prevalence in the jails of 'jail-fever', a virulent form of typhus fever not present in continental prisons and attributed by modern authorities to the specially filthy state of the English prisons. It seems clear that credit for this unusually quick success in parliament of a reform proposal was largely due to Howard's care and skill in preparing and presenting his case.[1] This suggests that the history of reform in England in the eighteenth century might have been a great deal more impressive if there had been universities or other institutions where men could have been taught the skills and disciplines needed for effective planning of programmes requiring, for their successful technical application, professional knowledge and administrative imagination. Such training was in some measure already routine in German universities and elsewhere, but it went against the spirit of English governmental institutions and the incredible torpor of the ancient universities.

Systematic search would, I am sure, add somewhat to the meagre list known to me of individual proposals for reform in general and specific reforms in particular and thus qualify, in minor degree, the picture I have given of a dominating complacency with respect to the eighteenth-century *status quo*. In other countries, and in other periods of English history, earlier and later, utopian literature is a good place to look for evidence of the existence of current hopes for social change which it would have been embarrassing or even hazardous publicly to disclose in plain language. In the England of our period, however, such literature was scanty and unrevealing. In the days of the early Stuarts, utopianism was frowned upon by the Church as smacking of the Anabaptistical heresy of dreaming of a perfect state on this earth. In the eighteenth century it would have been frowned upon as smacking of a tendency towards secular 'enthusiasm'. I have found only three utopian items in our period which have much relevance for reformist thought. The anonymous *Free State of Noland* (London, 1696), in which I think I detect a Harringtonian flavour, concentrates on constitutional reform with a moderate equalitarian bias. James Burgh's *Account of...the Cessares* (1764), proposes the division of the commons and the wastes among the poor, subject to a moderate annual charge whose proceeds were to be given to those persons who thereby would lose their 'right of commoning', and proposes also that mines should be what we would now call 'nationalised'. Michael Woodhull's *The Equality of Mankind* (1765) was a poem which was anti-monarchical, anti-clerical, and unenthusiastic about the middle class, but it made no specific proposals. Woodhull's sardonic characterisation of the middle class may be of interest:

> Those motley Beings next in order place,
> .Whose wavering stations wear a doubtful face,
> Who, dragg'd by Fortune into middle Life,
> That vortex of malevolence and strife,
> Envying the Great, and scoffing at the mean,
> Now swoln with pride, now wasted with chagrin,
> Like Mahomat's unsettled ashes dwell,
> Midway suspended between Heaven and Hell.[1]

I have found in the century only one extreme English radical, Thomas Spence. In 1775 he proposed in a lecture in Newcastle a substantially equalitarian system of land tenure. He later was to attract many followers, and also some official persecution, by his republications of this lecture and by other publications advocating agrarian and political radicalism.[1] Henry Brooke, an Irishman who lived at times in England, in 1767 published a novel, *The Fool of Quality*, which contained a medley of mystical and other miscellaneous material, as well as reflections on society which included one of the early manifestations of the influence of Rousseau on British social thought. It is to me a strange book, but in it the author makes one of his characters utter some remarks of a genuinely radical and quite pre-Marxian nature. I cite as an example: 'I look upon the money amassed by the wealthy to have been already extracted from the earnings of the poor, the poor farmer, the poor craftsman, the hard-handed peasant, and the day labourer, whose seven children perhaps subsist on the milk of a couple of cows.'[2]

Jonathan Shipley, who seems to have been the most liberal and least conventional of the Anglican bishops of the time in his references to social issues, in a sermon of 1773 relating to the colonies expressed the hope that a less unequal social structure than the existing one in the homeland might, under different conditions, be established in the colonies: 'May not a method be invented of procuring some tolerable share of the comforts of life to those inferior useful ranks of men to whose industry we are indebted for the whole? Time and discipline may discover some means to correct the extreme inequalities of condition between the rich and the poor, so dangerous to the innocence and the happiness of both.'[3]

Adam Smith, of course, has outstanding claims to being an advocate of social reform, but except for his slashing attack on the settlement laws his major proposals for change were not especially directed at improvement of the relative economic status of the poor. David Williams, a dissenting clergyman, like Jonathan Shipley a friend of Benjamin Franklin, in an undeservedly neglected book, *Lectures on the Universal Principles and Duties of*

Religion and Morality (London, 1779), deals at length, in a moderately equalitarian and philosophically anarchistic tone somewhat anticipatory of William Godwin, with the proper economic and ethical relations between the social classes.

I have called your attention to nearly the sum of the English discussions in the century up to the 1770s encountered in my reading which I regard as being clearly social-reformist, expressly or by implication, with respect to the status of the 'labouring poor'. It is, I confess, not a large sum, and better-informed scholars can, I am sure, add to it. I remind you, however, that, to ease my task, I have withheld comment on the post-American-Revolution decades, which are much richer in social criticism, and have deliberately excluded from my coverage the works of Scots and Irishmen written in their local surroundings and for local audiences.

Our visual notions of the conditions in which the eighteenth-century English poor lived, especially as far as rural housing is concerned, point more to the picturesque than to the sordid. The eighteenth-century rural cottage, whether as externally observed in its surviving examples or as seen in contemporary prints or paintings, is invariably good to look at, but it is representative of a fraction only of the cottages of the time. The intentionally 'picturesque' cottages were, moreover, built ordinarily on the estates of substantial landlords, and owned, constructed, sited, and designed by them or their agents. We all continue to find them 'picturesque', but their beauty may have been, as in the case of a goodly apple rotten at the core, wholly external, and even this external beauty was created in the service of the landlord, as embellishment to his estate, and to some extent to the disservice of the occupants. It has been said, for instance, that the gables of these cottages used up precious space and their windows often were made never to open. Of the many pictures by the artist, George Morland, which feature the picturesqueness of the English countryside, one, entitled 'Happy Cottagers', shows a pair of sturdy and becomingly dressed adults, three buxom children, a cottage as background, a large tree embracing the house, and an elaborate hanging birdcage at the side of the cottage. The cottage itself is not clearly depicted. It may well represent a one-room shelter for five persons. But the ensemble does make a pretty, if somewhat idealised, picture. [1] Should, however, the fact, if it is a fact, that the one-room cottage had to serve five persons detract from our appreciation of its pleasing exterior? Were the conditions of the poor, moreover, then any better anywhere else? Except for reports by visitors from colonial America, who did find English poverty depressing, and for lack of enthusiasm on the part of visitors from the Continent about the climate and especially about sanitary conditions and the state of public facilities in general in the English towns, most visitors to England appear to have found the condition of the English working classes superior to what they were familiar with in their own countries. English visitors to the Continent, or to Scotland or Ireland, likewise found the conditions of the working classes superior at home to what they were elsewhere.

There has been in our own day, however, all-embracing appreciation often approaching infatuation with what we take to have been the material aspects of English eighteenth-century day-to-day life: church, domestic and public architecture, gardens, interior decorating, paintings, carriages, saddle horses, silver and porcelain, clothing, and so on. It would perhaps contribute to a more balanced picture of the century if we keep in mind that, as in the case of the rural cottages of the poor, the things of beauty and of ease and comfort in the main existed for the service and delectation of the upper classes, and that in the main they were things to be constructed and cleaned and brushed and dusted and repaired by the poor for their superiors rather than to be possessed and enjoyed by themselves. John Chamberlayne, year after year in his year-book, *The State of Great Britain*, had an entry, 'The meanest mechanics and husbandmen want not silver spoons and some silver cups in their houses'.[1] I have often wondered whether we should take his word for those silver spoons and cups. But what of it? Even if they were really only pewter, some of us would still be envious.

I resist deliberately and determinedly, moreover, giving expression to any urge I may be subject to to assert obligations of the eighteenth century to conform to your—or to my—standards of social justice, of freedom, of beauty. Were I to take as seriously all I read in our very literary reviews about the sad cultural predicament we are in to-day as I take the current official reports on the economic condition of our own lower classes up to, say, the 20 per cent line, I should have to conclude that the only ethical superiority that our comfortable classes can claim as compared to eighteenth-century England is that we do have, and even systematically cultivate, a guilty social conscience in relation to the poor. I am not unaware, moreover, that not a few American academic aficionados of the literature of the English Augustan Age find a satisfying substitute for a sense of social guilt in the virtuous weeping of the Augustan literati. They shed their tears very publicly in the cemeteries over tombstones selected at random and in the contemplation of death at large, rather than in the slums as a response to the misery of living poor. But, if there is virtue in tear-shedding, *per se*, why boggle at where they chose to practice it? And was it not a credit to the age that authors could so successfully move their audiences to weep copiously, even if it was only in response to the exhibition of anguish by characters in plays or novels?

I have met few professional students of the English eighteenth century, aside from its theology and its bishops, who were not devoted admirers of not only those aspects of the century with which they were professionally occupied, but of the century as a whole, lock, stock, and barrel. Naturally, therefore, I have premonitions that you have found the enthusiasm expressed in this paper for the English eighteenth century too muted, and my love for it excessively dissembled. If I should nevertheless plead my love for it, it might provoke your saying about me in relation to the eighteenth century what George Eliot made Tom Tulliver say about himself in relation to birds: 'I'm fond of birds—that is, of throwing stones at them.' I would insist, however, that the England of the century we are discussing has always impressed me as a nearly perfect gentleman's utopia. What more can be asked of a commentator on the eighteenth century who claims only to be an aspiring scholar, and who happens to think that a scholar, as distinguished from a gentleman, or from a moraliser, must strive to escape acquiring the habit of appraising a past century in terms of the extent to which it conforms to his own values, preferences, tastes, and moral sentiments? In any case, even the saintly Thomas More's *Utopia* had slaves in it. A guest at a dinner party in Brussels during the French Revolution remarked that he admired the *Ancien Régime* except for its abuses. His émigré hostess exclaimed: 'Les abus! Mais c'est ce qu'il y avait de mieux.' 'The abuses! Why they were its best part!'[1] I do not approve of going quite that far, for in moral matters I am a historical relativist of what is perhaps a peculiar kind. I believe that each century except one's own has a right to its abuses, but that no century has an obligation to condemn, to praise, or to offer apologies for, another century's lapses from perfection.

CHAPTER 3

THE CHURCHMAN

by G. R. Cragg

Seldom has the religious man seemed to be so happily at home in society as in eighteenth-century England. He occupied a place which was always recognised and often honoured. Church and State, in intimate association, worked together in an alliance which was usually inequitable but which was seldom dishonourable. The bishop in his palace and the rector in his parsonage were an integral part of the social scene. Indeed, it is sometimes a great deal easier to define the social role of a churchman than it is to identify his religious convictions. But long before the century ends we begin to encounter a wholly different spirit. No longer can we question either the reality or the intensity of the religious experience of many Englishmen. In some instances we may wonder what relevance (if any) this earnest soul-searching had to the problems of society, but we cannot question its intensity or its importance.

It is tempting but dangerous to impose simple patterns on the complex phenomena of history. But for purposes of exposition it may be permissible to examine, first, the involvement of religious man in the social and political patterns of the earlier part of the century; and then to consider the revival, in the second half, of an emphasis on the faith and experience of the individual. But in both periods the dominant features were never exclusive. Bishop Hoadly, who was almost a caricature of a Hanoverian prelate, equated Christianity with a form of individualism so extreme that he virtually dissolved away the Church as a community of believers. But he was equally opposed to any intensity of religious

emotion, and William Law shrewdly twitted him with considering
'calmness and undisturbedness to be the ornament and defence of
human understanding in all its actions'.[1] At the opposite end of
the spectrum, both in time and in outlook, we encounter the
Evangelical anxiously feeling his spiritual pulse and lovingly
noting all his symptoms, but equally we have William Wilberforce campaigning for the abolition of slavery and Hannah More
struggling to improve the lot of the rural poor.

It was natural that in the early part of the eighteenth century
the social involvements of the churchman should obscure all other
aspects of the religious life. The reaction against puritanism made
zeal of any kind suspect; intensity of conviction was the distin-
guishing mark of the fanatic and was consequently dismissed with
the damning epithet, 'enthusiasm'. The influence of Locke and
Newton, fortified by the Deistic controversy, so emphasised the
role of reason that rationalism became 'a habit of thought ruling
all minds'.[2] Religion was acknowledged to be a suitable subject for
debate; it was not regarded as a normal ingredient in vivid personal
experience. The conventions of the day assured it an appropriate
place in the social pattern, and even its harshest critics acknowledged its practical advantages. Anthony Collins, the deist, always
sent his servants to church, to teach them (he said) not to rob
their master or to cut his throat. Lord Chesterfield, that cool and
sceptical observer of the social scene, treated religion with the
respect due to an important buttress of stability. 'Depend upon
this truth,' he wrote, 'that every man is the worse looked upon,
and the less trusted, for being thought to have no religion, in spite
of all the pompous and specious epithets he may assume, of *esprit
fort*, free thinker or moral philosopher; and a wise atheist (if such
a thing there is) would, for his own interest and character in the
world, pretend to some religion.'[3]

The emerging patterns of party politics combined with the
temper of the times to thrust the churchman firmly into the vortex
of political life. The House of Lords was still an important (often a

decisive) centre of power. Elections might change the complexion of the Commons; only death and the appointment of new bishops could affect the composition of the Lords. As party warfare became a settled feature of political life, the potential significance of the bishops became increasingly clear. Governments could be saved or overthrown by episcopal votes, as Walpole discovered (to his relief) in 1733.[1] Later ministers never forgot the lesson.

The bishops took relatively little part in the debates of the upper House. Wake had been a member for five years before he delivered his first speech. Warburton remarked that the bishops were usually too old when appointed to master the arts of political oratory. Moreover, their advanced age meant that changes in the bench were always imminent. It was quickly established (at least in the eyes of the politicians) that a bishop was primarily appointed to support a certain party.[2] The duke of Newcastle saw more clearly than anyone else the extent to which churchmen could be involved in the intricacies of party politics: beyond any of his rivals he was able to organise the potentialities latent in the Church connection into a massive system of political manipulation. No false reticence prevented him from making perfectly clear to aspiring clergymen the implications of promotion. They were expected to attend faithfully in the House and to vote invariably for the minister who promoted them. Their behaviour was closely watched and reproof speedily descended upon any bishop who let his private convictions deflect him from the narrow path of party loyalty. Even when he fell from power, Newcastle still hoped to hold his appointees to a strict obedience, and his demands then created an intolerable dilemma for the bishops whom he had elevated to the bench. Fidelity to him meant opposition to the ministers in power, and this automatically destroyed all immediate prospects of advancement. Archbishop Drummond and Bishop Yonge tried to reconcile the conflicting claims of loyalty and prudence by absenting themselves from the House, but Newcastle would not accept this evasion of responsibility. And, to add a further complication to a delicate position, there was always the possibility that a fallen minister might return to office.

Newcastle, of course, did not achieve his results merely by a watchful eye and a cautionary reprimand. He could enforce discipline because of the wide disparity between the incomes of various sees. At Canterbury or Durham, even at London or Winchester, a bishop could live like a prince, but at Bristol or Oxford he had indigence entailed upon him. The leaders of both parties seized the weapon which this placed in their hands. Initially they appointed men to the poorer sees; then, on proof of good behaviour, the bishop might begin the slow climb towards the rewards of unwavering loyalty.

Even the eighteenth-century politicians conceded that bishops had other tasks besides voting for their patrons in parliament. But the demands entailed in this kind of political obligation made it almost impossible for bishops adequately to discharge their primary religious duties. For a good part of each year they had to be in London—with the financial burden of maintaining a residence in the capital as well as an episcopal palace in the provinces—and even when they retired to their sees they could not escape their political responsibilities. They were expected to cultivate the men of consequence; a conscientious bishop would be on dining terms with all the leading gentry of the county. Social contacts would be used to canvass political support. When a crucial election was impending and the outcome seemed to be in doubt, the bishop was expected to throw all the weight of the ecclesiastical organisation behind his patron's candidate. Thus, in the Bedfordshire election of 1708, William Wake, then bishop of Lincoln, responded to the minister's appeals by urging his archdeacon to marshal all the forces of the Church to support the duke of Bedford's choice. The archdeacon had no scruples about using the Church's influence for political ends; actually he suggested a strategy much subtler than that which the bishop had devised, and in due course proved that he could apply it with success. Similarly in the Sussex election of 1734, Bishop Hare used all the persuasion he could command to swing the clerical support behind the candidates of the duke of Newcastle. In both cases, the polls suggested that the influence of the Church was a factor which politicians were foolish to ignore.

The place of the bishops in parliament was the symbol of their intimate involvement in the political life of the age. They reached this position by the hard and uncertain ladder of promotion. Advancement was often dependent on access to the right patron, and, since patrons were usually swayed by political or social considerations, the churchman could never forget his involvement in the structure of the nation's life. The only way to climb was to solicit the good offices of those with influence. The death of an incumbent—almost any incumbent—precipitated an inglorious stampede to secure the vacant place.[1] An eager candidate would hover in the anteroom of an expiring bishop till the breath was out of the episcopal body, and then post through the night to bear the news in person and claim the position. Sometimes he hoped that a letter might state his case with greater urgency. 'I think it my duty to acquaint your Grace', wrote Thomas Newton to the duke of Newcastle, 'that the archbishop of York lies a-dying, and, as all here think, cannot possibly live beyond to-morrow morning, if so long; upon this occasion of two vacancies, I beg, I hope, I trust your Grace's kindness and goodness will be shown to one who has long solicited your favour.'[2] The note of urgency was natural; contenders were many and the rewards were few. Hurd, writing to Warburton, mentioned that 'an old acquaintance of mine, Mr Caryl of Jesus, after many years of solicitation, has at length got a poor prebend from the Duke of Newcastle'.[3] Newcastle, indeed, was the first person to elevate ecclesiastical patronage from a questionable abuse to an intricate art. No living was too small to have a place in his elaborate designs. In translating a bishop he often stipulated that any presentations falling due would be surrendered into his hands.[4] High office, it was said, is a pyramid; only eagles or reptiles can reach its summit. New-castle's system unduly encouraged the reptiles. Fortunately a few eagles managed to reach the heights.

This kind of involvement with society encouraged worldliness. Perhaps the most savage indictment of the eighteenth-century Church is Hogarth's damning portrait of Bishop Hoadly. 'The lust of the flesh, the lust of the eyes, and the pride of life' have seldom been depicted with such merciless candour. Edmund Pyle, who lived with Hoadly, feared that the rich fare at the episcopal table might ruin his health, but he courageously ran the risk.[1] Pyle, of course, was well aware of the compensations that accrued to a man called to move in high ecclesiastical circles, and which outweighed any hazards incidental to such a life. He him-self did not aim at the most lucrative positions. He was content to be a prebendary, and he keenly savoured the advantages of a preferment which was dignified without being too exalted—and which was very pleasant. 'The life of a prebendary', as he confided to his *Memoirs*, 'is a pretty easy way of dawdling away one's time; praying, walking, visiting, and as little study as the heart could wish.'[2] An elderly dean of Westminster, feeling his end approach-ing, left in verse a *Nunc Dimittis* which is a perfect picture of a comfortable cleric growing old in happy indolence. 'I find me,' he concludes, 'I find me gently tending to decay.'[3]

The problems created by this pattern of social and political involvement were, of course, much more tangible than the temper which tended to pervade the Church. When competition for place became a professional necessity, pluralism was the inevitable sequel. This abuse was not the creation of the eighteenth century. It was a relic of medieval times. It had been practised with scarcely a twinge of conscience by the Caroline divines. But in the eighteenth century the scramble for places became more intense, and the rewards of success more spectacular. Moreover, we must remember that in the eighteenth century the scions of noble houses again begin to appear in the ranks of the 'dignified clergy', and an age acutely conscious of the gradations of nobility assumed that a peer's son could rightly hold more places of profit than a commoner. Brownlow North, the younger half-brother of Lord North, demonstrated what a man with high connections could sometimes accomplish. He became a canon of Christ Church at the age of twenty-seven. Two years later he was given the deanery of Canterbury. When thirty he was consecrated as bishop of Lichfield. A society which was normally very tolerant about such things was startled by such rapid advancement, but Lord North silenced any murmurs by pointing out that if Brownlow waited for promotion till he reached a more appropriate age he might no longer have a prime minister as a brother. But, since Lord North remained in office, Brownlow's progress was not arrested. At the age of thirty-three he was translated to Worcester, and seven years later to the wealthy see of Winchester. There he remained for thirty-nine years, and had at his disposal a certain amount of patronage which he bestowed on the members of his family. He made his elder son Master of St Cross Hospital, his younger son a prebendary of Winchester, and his grandson the registrar of the diocese. The latter office was a sinecure; the recipient was seven years old.[1] Satirists might attack pluralists and climbers, but the strain of worldliness both in society and in the Church meant that the judgment passed on those who tried and succeeded was not so harsh as the ridicule heaped on those who tried and failed. The inevitable consequence of pluralism was non-residence, and the two, in combination, created the bitter problems of the clerical underworld. The hopelessness and poverty of the curate who starved on £15 a year (or less) form the sad undertone in all sensitive contemporary comment on the life of the Hanoverian church.

In spite of much complacent acceptance of the Church's entanglement in social affairs, the abuses which the prevailing system both created and aggravated led in thoughtful men to a deep vein of pessimism. In the advertisement to his *Analogy* and in his 'Charge to the Clergy of the Diocese of Durham' Bishop Butler spoke in the most sombre terms of the predicament of the Church of England. The faith was ridiculed; aggressive unbelief was rampant. Indeed, rumour asserted that Butler was offered the primacy and declined it; the process of decay, he said, had proceeded too far for him to hope to arrest it.[1]

On the other hand there were many who regarded the Church's involvement in social and political affairs as both natural and right. It was an accepted fact which was buttressed by a carefully elaborated theory. Early in the century, Bishop Hoadly advanced extreme claims on behalf of the right of the State to control the Church,[2] and, though Tory churchmen raised angry outcries about Byzantine erastianism, they themselves proposed no viable alternative. Bishop Atterbury, indeed, had tried to do so. In precipitating the convocation controversy, he had insisted that the church possessed a large measure of independence. But Wake and Gibson, with the aid of White Kennett and others, had shown that Atterbury's position rested on a foundation of very shoddy scholarship. 'That Christian princes have a right not only to exercise authority over ecclesiastical persons,' wrote Wake, 'but to interpose in the ordering of ecclesiastical affairs too, neither our own articles and canons nor the consent of the universal church, ever since the empire became Christian, will suffer us to doubt.'[3] 'And I need not say', he added, 'that Christianity came not to usurp upon the civil power, but rather to engage men to be the more ready to undertake that duty which they owe to it.'[4] Wake's historical analysis of 'the doctrine taught by all English divines since the Reformation'[5] paved the way for Warburton's *Alliance*: the major eighteenth-century effort to delineate the relation between Church and State and to justify its existing pattern. He postulated a compact between two types of corporate body. The Church and State each needed the other; neither was really capable of functioning satisfactorily if dependent on its own resources. This hypothetical alliance was admittedly incapable of verification—and Lowth (in the suavest but most biting piece of controversial writing that the age produced) twitted Warburton on the impossibility of proving what he postulated[1]—but, after all, Warburton's theory was as plausible as the popular accounts of a contractual origin of the State. But this ingenious explanation of the interdependence of Church and State was needlessly hypothetical in order to account for the existing relationship, and by the end of the century William Paley was content to justify the establishment on purely utilitarian grounds.

The churchman was deeply involved in the life of the State, and the theorists had found an explanation to justify the situation. But, beyond the scope of politics, churchmen often had a more informal and more beneficial contact with society. In the Hanoverian age Anglicanism may largely have forfeited its prophetic function. It may have become too much a part of the corporate life to denounce its faults—or even to see them. But no one can complain that it was divorced from the experience of the people. George Crabbe might deplore the fox-hunting parson, but no one could object that the offender held himself aloof from the activities of the parish.[2] In describing Dr Taylor of Ashbourne, Boswell remarked approvingly that 'his size, and figure, and countenance, and manner, were that of a hearty English Squire, with the parson super-induced'.[3] In his own person Taylor symbolised a tie which Boswell deeply valued. The landowner and the rector lived and worked in a partnership which dealt with many of the problems of the parish. In Woodforde's *Diary of a Country Parson* the nature of the association is reflected on almost every page. The squire and the parson were in constant contact with each other. 'I dined, supped and spent the evening at Justice Creed's,' reports Woodforde; 'with him, his father and Mr Hindley...They behaved very respectively towards me.' He and his niece had dinner with the Squire's family: 'they behaved very civil and friendly towards us'. He noted that his friend and fellow-cleric, Du Quesne, in the orbit of a much more distinguished and important family, 'fretted

The Churchman

himself about being so tied by the leg, in dancing backward and forward to Townshends with his great company', and Woodforde remarked 'that being with our equals is much more agreeable'. So he joined a dining club of the gentry in his neighbourhood, carefully recorded the enormous meals they fed each other, participated with circumspection in the politics of the area, and showed considerable tact in reconciling the quarrels of his friends and neighbours. But he was always accessible to the humbler members of his parish. He entertained the older people to Christmas dinner. On St Thomas's day he received all the poor of the village and gave them 6d. apiece. When he held his tithe dinner he noted that there was 'much jollity throughout the afternoon and evening'. Their ways were often his ways. He bought tea from a smuggler, and was anxious about the noise the fellow made—though, apparently, he was little troubled by the ethics of the transaction.[1] And (the most striking feature of it all) there is scarcely a comment in the whole book to suggest that Woodforde was a man of any religious conviction or experience.

We must remember, however, that Woodforde's lapses about smuggled tea were not really characteristic either of the man himself or of the church which he served. Both the Tractarians and the Evangelicals despised the Hanoverians and deplored their lack of genuine religious concern. Their own presuppositions blinded them to one of the unquestioned elements of strength in the eighteenth-century church. Because they were deeply involved in the life of society, the Hanoverians were sensitive to the social problems of their age. They might express this concern in ways which their successors branded as mere moralism, but the eighteenth century needed to be reminded of ethical standards, and the leaders of the Church spoke frankly on problems whose seriousness was admitted on every hand. Court masquerades were regarded as an open incitement to promiscuity. That was why Wake and Gibson objected to them so strongly. Few denied that gin was demoralising the new urban proletariat. Hogarth's 'Gin Lane' was

63

merely a particularly vivid portrayal of a major problem. A churchman like Secker was not only aware of the issue; he was vigorous in demanding a remedy. This attitude was a legacy from Tillotson's carefully inculcated ethics; yet George Whitefield complained that Tillotson 'knew no more about religion than Mahomet'.[1] To the Tractarians it was deplorable that eighteenth-century sermons had so often been ethical rather than dogmatic in emphasis; but the Hanoverians believed that they lived in a licentious age, and they were convinced that their contemporaries needed to be confronted with the elementary claims of morality.

It is, of course, a caricature to present the eighteenth century as wholly devoid of personal religious concern. For many people Dr Johnson stands as the symbol of his age, as the epitome of its virtues, even as the incarnation of its defects. But everyone is aware of the quality of Dr Johnson's prayers. In his devotional writings he was obviously expressing a faith which he had found to be a buttress against the depression and the fears which so often beset him. Here is something that penetrates far beneath the surface gloss of an age which applauded classical elegance. In Warburton's correspondence we sometimes find that that very truculent controversialist could show wholly unexpected flashes of religious insight and even of Christian charity. Lord Chancellor Macclesfield seemed to his friend Dr Pearce 'to live under a constant sense of religion as a Christian: at his hours of leisure, reading and studying the holy Scriptures, more especially after his misfortunes had removed him from the business and fatigues of his office as Chancellor'.[2] The duke of Newcastle, who stands as the great architect of a system of church patronage—or is it political corruption?—betrayed at times an almost painful scrupulosity about partaking unworthily of Holy Communion. He found comfort in reading Tillotson's sermons, and considered them so helpful that he proposed to study them in greater detail. This may seem thin fare, suitable for a Hanoverian politician, but, in Bishop Hume's advice to Newcastle, we detect a note which is perhaps the best part of eighteenth-century religion. 'While we continue in this world,' wrote the bishop, 'we have a part to act in it, which cannot be carried on without engaging our thoughts and attention, but while these thoughts exclude not the thoughts and attention to another world, they are innocent and very consistent both with reason and religion, nor need we think ourselves bad Christians for being good citizens.'[1]

The early part of the century was preoccupied with the dry light of reason and with the sober obligations of ethical behaviour. Because this emphasis did not satisfy the whole man a reaction was inevitable. By 1738, John Wesley had 'felt his heart strangely warmed', and that phrase has too often obscured the fact that in many respects he remained a typical eighteenth-century cleric, concerned with education, scholarship, sound theology and (usually) sound sense. But he discovered for himself the importance of experience and the power of emotion, and with the aid of these he proved that he could achieve phenomenal results among the neglected and often brutalised populace in the new towns. Wesley was concerned with the individual and proposed to change him. He did not leave his converts as they had been, nor did he let them remain in isolation. He gathered his followers into societies. He divided the societies into 'classes'. He devised a whole series of means whereby his members could serve each other, find their proper place in society and so serve the world about them. He early discovered that 'the Bible knows nothing about solitary religion'.[2] He never tired of emphasising that 'the Gospel of Christ knows of no religion but social; no holiness but social holiness'.[3] He never fell into the preoccupation with the individual and his emotions which marked a great deal of later revivalism. This, I believe, was a consequence of the way he interpreted experience. He was concerned with what happened to people, and he knew that people are always placed in a social context. We may hazard the surmise that Wesley's results were a good deal more permanent than Whitefield's because he conceived of man's experience in a much more comprehensive way.

Wesley and Whitefield, who agreed on so many things, disagreed about theology. Wesley was an Arminian, Whitefield a Calvinist (of sorts). Many of the best-known leaders of the Evangelical movement in the Church of England were more akin to Whitefield than to Wesley. Among them we find a stress on vital experience often leading to an extreme preoccupation with the individual and his states of feeling. James Hervey (a pupil of Wesley's at Lincoln College, Oxford) wrote a series of meditations in which sentimentality balances precariously between the maudlin and the pathological. The reader of *Meditations among the Tombs* is aghast at their mood and bewildered by their popularity, but A. M. Toplady (author of 'Rock of Ages') speaks of their author as 'the seraphic Mr Hervey'. Most of the Evangelicals began their religious careers with the crisis of conversion. Before, all was sin; afterwards, all was grace. The wonder of the new experience led to constant dwelling on the individual. This did not obscure the duty of reaching others, but it did not always lead to any awareness of the need to create a redeemed society out of the converted individuals. The Tractarians complained (with some justification) that the Evangelicals had no adequate doctrine of the Church. It might be added that some of them had no sufficient concern with society. Toplady's *Diary* is an anxious record of the states of his own soul. 'I cannot help noting to my shame', he observes, 'and as a mark of my exceeding depravity that after all the Lord's Sabbath-day mercies to me yesterday, I was never, that I know of, more cold, lifeless and wandering than I was in secret prayer last night, just before going to bed.' But a couple of pages later the mood has changed. 'I was all on fire for God, and the fire, I verily believe, caught from heart to heart. I am astonished, when I review the blessings of this Lord's day. That a sinner so vile, so feeble, so ill and so hell-deserving should be thus carried beyond himself and be enabled to preach with such demonstration of the Spirit!'[1]

To the Evangelical, formalism and apathy were the cardinal faults of conventional Christians. 'These people call themselves children of God,' remarked John Flavel, 'but their piety comprises nothing [so] personal or particular, nothing which [so much] distinguishes them from the heedless world...'[1] The classic protest against nominal Christianity—and one of the earliest of religious best-sellers—was William Wilberforce's *A Practical View of the Prevailing Religious System of Professed Christians*. A religion of form had produced a society marked by 'sober sensuality, sober avarice, sober ambition', but also by competition and display. Wilberforce left no doubt as to the pattern of earnest zeal which he recommended. But this was not piety warming itself before its private glow. Christian devotion, he claimed, issued in a life of concern for others, and this brought him in due course to a careful exposition of the effectiveness of true religion as a means of creating a good society. After a detailed exposition of these results he sums up his argument with the words, 'such are the blessed effects of Christianity upon the temporal well-being of political communities'.[2] Wilberforce's picture is generalised and is lacking in specific details. In this respect it is a far cry from the atmosphere of the House of Commons and the campaign for the abolition of the slave trade. It was here that Wilberforce and his Evangelical friends gave effect to their conviction that a faith concerned with personal piety may nevertheless 'produce good effects in society'.[3] As Isaac Milner, the president of Queens' College, Cambridge, observed in a letter to Wilberforce, 'if you carry this point in your whole life, that life will be far better spent than in being prime minister many years'.[4]

The same balance between faith and works, zeal and action, can also be seen in the career of Hannah More. When converted she was a woman of wealth and prominence, with a secure position in society and a modest but genuine literary success behind her. Once awakened to the possibilities of a new life, she addressed herself to the world she had known so well. In her *Thoughts on the*

Importance of the Manners of the Great to General Society she attacked the prevailing obsession with cards and gambling, and she had an appreciable effect on social customs. Gradually she became aware of the problems of a stratum of national life about which she had previously known nothing. William Wilberforce pointed out to her the conditions which prevailed in the villages of the Mendip Hills. The labourers were ignorant as well as poor; the more substantial farmers were overbearing and despotic; the clergy were indolent, indifferent and often non-resident. To combat the prevailing ignorance and vice, Hannah More and her sister established schools, first for children, then for adults. At every turn they encountered opposition bred of ignorance, superstition and fear. The courage of these women, as well as their enlightened and disinterested zeal, reflected the evangelical spirit in its most attractive guise. Nor must we forget that the latter part of the eighteenth century has appropriately been called 'the age of charity'. Behind such enterprises as charity schools, hospitals and foundling homes, was a desire to translate personal conviction into appropriate social forms.

In the eighteenth century religion had held in uncertain equipoise the competing claims of the individual and his society. As the age drew to its close Burke temporarily fused them into one. With scathing ridicule he attacked the abstract theorists who misconceived man's nature because they isolated him from the creative social forces which make him what he is. 'This sort of people', he said, 'are so taken up with their theories about the rights of man that they have totally forgotten his nature.'[1] History and the moral order provide the necessary context; instinct, feeling, concrete reason, the familiar patterns into which time builds our deepest emotions, all presuppose a life closely unified and integrated with the lives of others. In this creative process the formative power is provided by religion, 'for we know, and it is our pride to know, that man is by his nature a religious animal'.[2] Organic growth, which fashioned human societies, had knit their essential components into the unity of a nation's life. The English people, he claimed, 'do not consider their church establishment as convenient, but as essential to their state...Church and state are ideas inseparable in their minds, and scarcely is the one ever mentioned without mentioning the other'.[1] Burke's account of the free and honoured place of the Church was written by a politician who must have observed the working of the eighteenth-century system but who reported in a highly selective way what he saw. Even in the abuses of Church life he was able to discover virtues, and possibly the light in which he placed them made it easier for the succeeding century to reform them.

At times the eighteenth century had exaggerated, to the point of caricature, the intimate involvement of the churchman in the nation's life. It had recovered, with the danger of a parallel distortion, a sense of the vital importance of the religious man's experience. It is appropriate that the period should end with Burke's ringing declaration of the creative unity in which man, an essentially religious being, finds his proper place in society by the creative traditions of an historic faith. The Church, which is the spiritual home of the people, must be involved in every aspect of the nation's life. 'We will', he exclaimed, 'have her mixed throughout the whole mass of life, and blended with all the classes of society.'[2]

CHAPTER 4

THE ARTIST

by Rudolf Wittkower

Vasari records that in the early sixteenth century there existed painters in Florence who were at odds with society. He did not mince words in characterising their behaviour. 'They lived like swine and brute beasts'—he writes—'they never washed their hands, nor their faces or hair or beards; they did not sweep their houses and never made their beds . . . they drank only from the bottle or jug; and this miserable existence of theirs, living, as the saying goes, from hand to mouth, was held by them to be the finest in the world.'[1] The artist alienated from the rest of mankind had made his entry.

But it was only during the nineteenth and early twentieth centuries that great numbers of artists chose to step outside the pale of society, as if driven by a relentless force. We are all familiar with the type: the outsider, the neurotic genius, the nonconformist and eccentric, who by his behaviour, his habits, his opinions and even his dress deliberately tried to shock those on whose bounty he had to live.

Between the mid-sixteenth century and the dawn of the romantic era there lay a long period of conformity: more or less successfully, artists were striving to be at peace with the world. Of course, the 'proto-bohemian' type of artist, first traceable in sixteenth-century Florence, never disappeared entirely. From a long list of distinguished names I recall Caravaggio and Adriaen Brower, Frans Hals and the Italo-French Jean-Nicolas Servandoni, who also worked in London and of whom Diderot said that he 'had fifteen thousand ways of accumulating wealth and thirty thousand of spending it'.[2]

The Artist

No such figures appear among British artists of the eighteenth century. If we exclude Blake, who opens a new epoch, British artists of the period here under review were conformists who fought for physical survival and social recognition. They endeavoured to secure a livelihood and improve their status in a rapidly changing society. This is also true of Hogarth, the only great artist of the period who embarked in social criticism and in castigating the mores of society.

Some of you may expect a paper dealing with an analysis of the message conveyed by 'Four Stages of Cruelty', 'A Harlot's Progress', 'A Rake's Progress', 'Industry and Idleness', 'Gin Lane' and the 'Marriage-à-la-Mode', and I admit the justification of such an interpretation of my task. But, first, my principal commentator, Professor Paulson, is much better equipped than I am to contribute this aspect to the topic; and, in addition, it might be argued that Hogarth was a *social critic* who conveyed his message mainly through the medium of engravings. The opinions he voiced as a *professional artist* for the benefit of professional artists are a different matter, and it is these that I shall discuss in a wider context.

Taking the artists as a professional group, and not as individual citizens or social and moral philosophers, I cannot but suggest a volte-face of the argument because 'Society versus the Artist' (rather than 'The Artist versus Society') is the recurrent eighteenth-century theme and the remedy of this situation was the most urgent concern of British artists.

Some passages in Jonathan Richardson's *An Essay on the Theory of Painting*, published in 1715, take us right to the core of the problem. He bluntly states that painters are not regarded as gentlemen and that 'the Word *Painter* does not generally carry with it an Idea equal to that we have of other Professions...'.[1] Moreover, he analyses the reasons for the profession's inferiority. If a gentleman, he argues, has a knowledge of the theory of painting it adds to his aura of cultural attainment. And it is not unworthy of him if he adds the mechanical side to the theory and himself paints for his pleasure without any reward. The source of all the trouble, therefore, seems to be—he concludes—that painters work for money, 'and if this has something Low and Servile in it, we must take our place amongst Men accordingly'.

However, he shrewdly observes, to take money for employment is not dishonourable. In fact, the painter is in the good company of all those who 'receive Money for the Exercise of their Abilities of Body or Mind'. Thus Richardson disposes of a prejudice derived from the supposedly mercenary character of the profession. But he also insists that the unbiased acceptance of the profession is dependent on the artist's conduct. He invites artists to avoid 'all Low, and Sordid Actions and Conversation, all Base and Criminal Passions...The way to be an Excellent Painter, is to be an Excellent man', and such a man 'may be placed amongst those whom all the World allow to be Gentlemen, or of Honourable Employments, or Professions'.

Richardson was, of course, not aware that he reiterated demands current in Italy from the mid-sixteenth century onward. To project an image of the artist as a highly educated, well-bred, versatile man of the world had long appeared the wherewithal to achieve full recognition—and sometimes the acceptance of an immaculate code of behaviour bore the desired results. Just as continental artists before them, so British eighteenth-century artists desperately tried to ape high-class society, even those who had a solid bourgeois background and rose to the top of the profession. Reynolds and Wilson were sons of clergymen; Allan Ramsay was the son of a well-known writer; Gainsborough's father was a prosperous cloth-merchant; Nathaniel Dance inherited a fortune and married an exceedingly wealthy widow; Stubbs's father was a surgeon and Stubbs himself, the famed author of *The Anatomy of the Horse* (1766), was a first-rate natural scientist besides being a first-rate painter. Nevertheless, the need for self-assertion was constantly felt, for galling experiences, also on the

The Artist

Continent, were not uncommon. In 1755 Robert Adam reported from Rome about Mrs Ramsay that 'being the wife to an artist prevents her being admitted into any company'[1]—and this although she was the granddaughter of a Scottish peer, Lord Stormont.

Robert Adam, the scion of a most successful Scottish architect, following the maxim that the dress makes the man, donned expensive fashionable clothes in Paris from silk stockings to a velvet suit, a gold-handled sword and a large hat with a white feather; he must have looked like a French dandy. Although the masquerade often served its purpose, he also had to face humiliating rebuffs; thus the British ambassador, Lord Albemarle, never received him.[2] Reynolds, at the height of his career, not only committed most of his savings to the purchase of a house in London's fashionable Leicester Square, but also owned a carriage with carved and gilt wheels and panels painted by the most eminent coach-painter of his day. Northcote, Reynolds's pupil, recorded Miss Reynolds's (Sir Joshua's sister's) complaint that the carriage was too showy, but Reynolds rejoined: 'What, would you have one like an apothecary's carriage?'[3] Reynolds's mild form of exhibitionism had a tradition in England: there had been a long line of court-painters who enjoyed special privileges, drew large salaries, attained the highest honours and were accepted by high society, but they all were foreigners, from Antonio Mor to Vandyck, Peter Lely and Godfrey Kneller. Sir Peter Lely kept several servants and footmen. 'He always had the table laid for twelve, and his friends as well as foreigners who had dealings with him were invited to partake. Meanwhile there was music and singing in another room.'[4] Sir Godfrey kept a coach and six, had a large town-house with liveried servants and an ample country-seat, and—as Rouquet, the Swiss miniature painter and enameller, informs us[5]—his 'pleasant conversation finely entertaining when a-painting' and the facility of his performance were the praise of one recognised as an equal. Such artists lived, of course, at peace with society and vice versa. But they were the exceptions. The great mass of artists was in desperate straits and their dilemma had more than one cause.

Let me tell a significant anecdote reported of the first Queen Elizabeth. As a new-year's gift to her, Dr Symson, the dean of the Queen's Chapel, surprised her with a Common Prayer-book interleaved with engravings representing the lives and martyr-doms of the saints. The Queen took the dean severely to task:

'You know I have an aversion to idolatry, to images, and pictures of this kind—I pray, Mr Dean, how came you by these pictures? Who engraved them?' 'I know not who engraved them—I bought them.' 'From whom bought you them?' 'From a German.' 'It is well it was from a stranger. Had it been from any of our subjects, we should have questioned the matter.'[1]

Her aversion prevailed and history painting, regarded on the Continent as the only task worthy of the elevated painter, an opinion supported by a closely-knit classical theory, remained proscribed in Protestant England well into the eighteenth century.

Portraiture—or face-painting, as it was called in England—had been and remained the traditional occupation of British artists. A man like Jonathan Richardson, who, with other Englishmen before and after him, believed in the validity of the classical doctrine and the supreme importance of history painting—which the British artist was scarcely given a chance to practise—tried to resolve this delicate problem by theoretically elevating the face-painter to the level of the history-painter. His claim is condensed in the following passage:

To be a good Face-Painter, a degree of the Historical and Poetical Genius is requisite, and a great Measure of the other Talents and Advantages which a good History-Painter must possess...A Portrait-Painter must understand Mankind, and enter into their Characters, and express their Minds as well as their Faces: And as his Business is chiefly with People of Condition, he must Think as a Gentleman, and a Man of Sense...[2]

A generation later Reynolds translated theory into practice by portraying many of his sitters in the poses of famed antique statues and of well-known figures in Renaissance paintings.[1]

But the rank and file of artists were far removed from considerations of this kind. They tried to eke out a precarious livelihood with a type of face-painting that often did not rise above the level of a popular craft. Many had to supplement their income by decorating carriages and painting shop-signs. Through the seventeenth and the early eighteenth centuries, at a time when the power of the guilds had been broken in France and Italy, English face-painters, coach-painters and house-painters were all equally ranked as tradesmen and organised in the Painter-Stainers Company.

These artists felt cornered and those who had higher aspirations did not know how to break out of the vicious circle. It is true, however, that as a rule their intellectual and professional standards were disgraceful, and one can hardly blame the aristocratic virtuoso, back from his grand tour to Italy, for regarding them as low-class practitioners and neglecting them.

The aristocratic patrons of the first half of the eighteenth century, themselves learned in the theory and practice of high art or at least recognising its distinction, were prepared to accept a 'native' artist equipped with a great deal of polite and theoretical knowledge outside his craft. These were the people from whom in the 1750s Reynolds with his elegant, easy and ample classical portraits was winning commission after commission. He himself, like the members of the recently founded Dilettanti Society, who were to be at once his friends and patrons, became a collector of the paintings and drawings of old masters—the 'black masters', as Hogarth dubbed them—and steeped himself in antique and sixteenth-century art, as a life-giving fount of inspiration.

As we have seen, for the majority of artists no such sunny prospects of advancement in their profession opened before them. They were tied to their shops and painting rooms and saw all avenues of patronage closed to them. They attributed their bad luck to the aristocratic fashion of investing enormous sums in forming collections of old masters, at the expense of an interest in modern, living artists. Often they were forced to scrape a livelihood by copying old masters for dealers. One of these painters later said that he and his fellows were 'generally speaking the property of picture dealers, their principal employers, and held by them in vassalage and dependence'.[1]

It was in the interest of these men that Hogarth was fighting. I suppose Richardson's somewhat esoteric argumentation did not catch his fancy. He took the bull by the horns and made it clear that moralising appeals to the upper classes had no chance of success. He shrewdly observed that the position in England was very different from that on the Continent.[2] Popery fostered history painting; English religion rejected it. The nobility preferred foreign pictures to native works. How, he asked, could anybody be expected to give 40 guineas for a modern landscape 'when he can purchase one, which, for little more than double the sum, shall be sanctioned by a sounding name, and warranted original by a solemn-faced connoisseur?' Most artists had to cater for the needs of people whose houses were too small to hold vast compositions. The English, he argued, are a commercial people. They are inclined, in any case, to encourage trade rather than painting and sculpture. What was there to induce a man to enter the business of art when 'his next-door neighbour, perhaps a porter-brewer or an haberdasher of smallwares, can without any genius accumulate an enormous fortune in a few years, become lord mayor or a member of Parliament, and purchase a title for his heir?'[3] And with a note of resignation he concludes that, since very few painters get even moderately rich, 'it is not reasonable to expect that they should waste their lives in cultivating the higher branch of the art until their country becomes more alive to its importance, and better disposed to reward their labours'. When he once mentioned this idea to a member of the Society for the Encouragement of Arts, Manufactures, and Commerce, he elicited the rejoinder: 'The poorer we keep the artists, the cheaper we might purchase their works.'

It is true, Reynolds and Gainsborough moved in the society of the great as equals, but Hogarth knew that this could never be the answer for the troubles of the majority of his fellows, whose only sphere of advancement was that of the industrious apprentice—to rise in trade from the workshop to the Mansion House.

Salvation, it seemed to many, lay in the foundation of an academy after the model of the French Academy established by Louis XIV in the mid-seventeenth century. They regarded a Royal Academy as the *deus ex machina*. An academy would provide a social and professional organisation on a level with other learned institutions; and titles and honours, important appendages to an academy, supplied status symbols which publicly acknowledged the divorce of the *artifex academicus* from the guild-controlled artisan. An academy, in short, not only would promote the intellectual and professional competence of its members, but would, above all, place the artist on a social level with his client and assure patronage. Later, Northcote regarded the rank of R.A. as 'equal to a patent of nobility'.

Some attempts had been made under James I, Charles I and even during the Commonwealth of establishing an academy of art in England,[1] but all were equally unsuccessful. British artists had to wait longer than those of any other country until their longing for an authoritative central institution and, implicitly, for social recognition was fulfilled. It was Kneller, the thriving foreigner, who first opened a private academy of art in London in 1711. After Kneller's death, in 1724, other competitive institutions sprang up, but their life was embittered by factions and jealousies. Nevertheless, they gave the students an opportunity of some academic training and embodied a flattering hierarchy with a Governor and Directors at the top, after the model of continental academies. In 1735 (after Sir James Thornhill's death), Hogarth took a lead in the affairs of these so-called academies, but characteristically sought to revert to an organisation closer to the old Craftsmen's Guilds. The outcome was the well-known St Martin's Lane Academy which was run on democratic lines, without presidents, directors and professors, for Hogarth was averse to pretensions which reminded him 'of the foolish parade of the French Academy'.[1] But, to quote from John Pye's *Patronage of British Art*, published in 1845,

when the aspirant stepped from his study...and looked around him, amidst the wealth and splendour of the metropolis of Great Britain, for the spirit of patriotic encouragement...he found reformed religion inculcating unadorned simplicity; a monarch on the throne with little propensity for refined pleasures; and, in natural consequence, native genius and cultivated intellect in art as entirely neglected as though they were useless alike to the well-being of the state and the dignity of man.[2]

Small wonder that, in spite of the success of the St Martin's Lane Academy, the craving for a Royal Academy following the French example steadily increased. At last, in 1755 a number of leading artists constituted themselves into a committee and published a charter for the establishment of such an academy. I quote from the revealing Introduction:

The prodigious sums England has laid out at foreign markets for paintings, is but a trifle compared to the more prodigious sums expended by English travellers for the bare sight of such things as they despaired of ever seeing at home. But the loss in point of money is not so much as in point of character; for we voluntarily yield the palm to every petty state that has produced a painter...one would think England the only country in the world incapable of producing one; as if the genius of a painter were one kind of essence, and the genius of a poet another; as if the air and soil that gave birth to a Shakespeare and a Bacon, a Milton and a Newton, could be deficient in any species of excellence whatsoever.[3]

The logic is, of course, fallacious. But the authors must have thought that the battle-cry 'British art for the British through the agency of a Royal Academy' could not fall on deaf ears. On the other hand, their proposals surely aroused some misgivings. Those who sponsored the charter, bitterly aware that something had to be done to improve their position, attributed the fault to the great. The great were infatuated with sham 'black masters'—then let us go, they argued, still higher and seek the protection of Majesty. But they were trying it both ways: like tradesmen they were trying to suppress the foreign competition of 'high art' while at the same time they strove, by royal patronage, to rise above the level of tradesmen and become polite practitioners of 'high art' themselves.

Reynolds was a member of the committee.[1] He was of course in favour of its declared purpose, the foundation of a Royal Academy; but one cannot help wondering whether he felt quite at ease, for he could hardly identify himself fully with the tenor of the committee's appeal. These artists' politics smelt of trade. He was rising on the tide of the prevailing aristocratic taste and could afford to keep aloof. Hogarth, on the other hand, was convinced that a Royal Academy would not solve the artists' dilemma and so he fought the idea tooth and nail. The real purpose of such an academy was, he declared, 'that a few bustling characters, who have access to people of rank, think they can thus get a superiority over their brethren, be appointed to places, and have salaries as in France for telling a lad when an arm or a leg is too long or too short'.[2] He knew that the patronage of the nobility offered little hope to the mass of struggling artists. Their salvation, he felt, was not above, but below. Those who thought that a Royal Academy would bridge the gulf between the working artists and their natural market were 'a band of profound blockheads'.

The scheme of 1755 came to nothing, not because of Hogarth's intervention but because the Dilettanti Society, the wealthy amateurs on whose financial support the success of the project depended, contrived to have a majority of votes constitutionally guaranteed and insisted on putting one of their group in the president's chair.[1] A dead end seemed to have been reached. In the event, it was unexpectedly overcome.

In 1739 the newly established Foundling Hospital was granted a royal charter. From the beginning Hogarth was an enthusiastic supporter of this charitable enterprise. He was also a close friend of its founder, Captain Coram. He painted Coram and presented the splendid portrait to the establishment in 1740. Soon other artists followed Hogarth's example and over the years the Hospital became a veritable gallery of contemporary British art that attracted large crowds of people of all classes.[2] This success with the general public led to the decision—taken in 1759 by a committee of sixteen leading artists[3]—to organise annual exhibitions. In the course of their deliberations they decided to approach Samuel Johnson with the request to correct a letter addressed to the Society for the Encouragement of Arts, Manufactures and Commerce[4] soliciting the use of the Society's great room in the Strand. The appeal was successful and on 21 April 1760 the exhibition was opened representing 69 artists with 131 works.

The artists were beginning to break down the division between themselves and the public by their own efforts rather than by appeals to the great; and consequently Hogarth lent them his support. When, the following year, the artists, constituted as the 'Society of Artists of Great Britain',[5] held their exhibition at Spring Gardens near Trafalgar Square, Hogarth supplied his famous frontispiece and tailpiece to the catalogue, the first of its kind. The frontispiece shows a fountain with water pouring from a lion's head, under the bust of the young King George III, who had ascended the throne in 1760. The water flows into a watering-can with which a personification of Britannia waters three young trees labelled 'painting', 'sculpture' and 'architecture'. The trees represent the fresh shoots of British art and we are given to understand that they cannot flourish unless they are nourished by dual patronage: royal munificence as well as the support of the whole of Britain. Hogarth, in other words, had illogically moved toward the acceptance of royal support, but he could surely identify himself with the new self-assured attitude of the artists and with the purpose of these exhibitions as set out in the preface to the Catalogue of 1762, once again supplied by Johnson's pen.[1] His rolling phrases culminate in the following passage:

...these men can never be accused [of envy or artifice], who, already enjoying all the honours and profits of their profession, are content to stand candidates for public notice, with genius yet unexperienced, and diligence yet unrewarded; who, without any hope of encreasing their own reputation or interest, expose their names and their works only that they may furnish an opportunity of appearance to the young, the diffident, and the neglected. The purpose of this Exhibition is not to enrich the Artists, but to advance the Art; the eminent are not flattered with preference, nor the obscure insulted with contempt; whoever hopes to deserve public favour is here invited to display his merit.

The majority of artists seemed fairly united and their public standing secure: more than one way opened leading to the foundation of the Royal Academy. But in the following years internecine strife among the artists had a retarding effect. Reynolds shunned involvement and only after all negotiations had been concluded surrendered to Benjamin West's strong representations and agreed to being elected President when the Academy was constituted on 10 December 1768, four years after Hogarth's death.

The opening of the Royal Academy coincided with social changes long in the making. England's ascendancy in trade and industry gave rise to a large and ambitious middle class with a patriotic pride in the nation's cultural achievement. The Foundling Hospital exhibitions had been a revealing pointer. It was mainly Hogarth who had conditioned this new public to taking an interest in the visual arts by turning—as he tells us in his autobiography—to 'painting and engraving modern moral subjects, a field not broken up in any country or any age...subjects that will both entertain and improve the mind, bid fair to be of the greatest utility, and must therefore be entitled to rank in the highest class...'.[2]

The different viewpoints of Reynolds and Hogarth had appeared irreconcilable: the one professed a learned and elevated art, the other a narrative, popular art; the one strode a path up to social recognition, the other down to the masses. But, strangely enough, long before the end of the century the gulf between these two approaches narrowed down considerably. Not only had Hogarth ennobled popular art, but academic artists had to abandon some of the lofty aims of 'high art' and seek popular approbation. The Academy had a royal charter but it had support neither from the Court nor from the State. Financially it was dependent on the annual exhibitions and consequently on the support given it by the large middle-class public. This public was moved by themes of national interest, up-to-date problems of moral conduct, social criticism, political, religious and personal satire, reportage and caricature—in other words, by the world opened up in Hogarth's prints. Northcote's verdict that 'all the heathen deities are a pack of wretches that would not be endured in any civilised society' shows to what extent the Royal Academicians were prepared to meet popular taste.

The new situation is thrown into strong relief by the rise of such men as John Boydell.[1] Boydell started his career as an engraver, later became Alderman and Lord Mayor of London and headed the British print-trade for almost fifty years (he died aged 85 in 1804). He had made true the tale of Hogarth's industrious apprentice; he had risen to the highest honours through industry and commerce, and at the summit of his life reconciled the taste of the general public with the ambitions of the academic artist. John Ireland, Hogarth's eighteenth-century biographer, said about him: 'Boydell awakened the spirit of historical and poetical painting in this country, and opened a mine of patronage that had been sought in vain from the nobility.'[2] This middle-class upstart seemed to have made good where royalty and nobility had failed. To be sure, in such company the artist was not lacking recognition.

In 1786 Boydell set on foot his project of having Shakespeare's plays illustrated in large paintings by a host of artists. Reynolds regarded it at first as below the dignity of the arts to enter into the service of speculation, but, not unexpectedly, he capitulated. The seal was set on the alliance between the middle-class patron and the Royal Academicians when, at the Academy dinner of 1789—in the year of the French Revolution, which was also the year of the opening of the Shakespeare Gallery—a toast was drunk to 'Alderman Boydell, the commercial Maecenas'.[1]

This anticlimactic toast symbolically resolved, at the end of the century, the old conflict between the artist and his patron—in a manner, however, utterly different from the artists' hopes and dreams at the beginning of the century, when Richardson spoke out for them.

I should have liked to release you on this note of a 'happy end', but history develops in circles rather than in a line ascending toward the common good. It is true that the annual Academy Exhibitions brought official art to the people. It is true that the exhibitions were regarded as a social event (which they still are) and that the artists had become an important power in the life of the metropolis. It is also true that for a short period almost all the artists of merit took a hand in the affairs of the Academy, that the great names in British art were united in its representative organisation and that Britain dictated the taste of Europe. And yet Hogarth's perceptive intuition of the merits or rather iniquities of such an institution proved correct.

According to the Academy's constitution only forty members and twenty associates were admitted. Non-members who exhibited in the Academy were not permitted to exhibit with any other Society nor were they admitted as candidates for election. As a result, other, private organisations of artists withered away. So, in actual fact, the leading artists formed a body of overseers, who conferred academic honours on themselves and the men of their choice, while the existence of the Academy added to the degradation of the many who were excluded from its membership.

Finally, we should not forget that, at the time the Academicians were hobnobbing with their commercial patron, a new type of artist began to turn both against the ideology vested in the Academy and the philistinism endemic in middle-class society.

CHAPTER 5

THE COMPOSER

by Paul Henry Lang

Because there are few periods in musical history so shrouded in misconception and misinterpretation as eighteenth-century England, a few remarks must precede our discussion.

Musical historiography has almost always treated stylistic and cultural departures as the exclusive achievement of individuals; one would think that music has nothing to do with the history of ideas. The material points of reference are, it is true, more difficult in music than in the other arts, and of course far more difficult to verbalise. But the cultural historian must deal with the difficult problem of the relationship between the individually developing arts. It is of considerable importance that he establish the characteristics shared by the several arts of a period, but he will go astray if he disregards the specific solutions demanded by each. Nor may he ignore the time-lag between the various arts of any given period; the architecture of an era may be in full decline when its music is just beginning to be in the ascendant. Finally, the hierarchy of the arts varies from time to time.

The continued existence or influence of older styles presents a specific difficulty to the music historian, for it is characteristic of music that its stylistic transformations are the slowest among the arts; and once a style becomes archaic it becomes far more so than do the other arts of the same period. For example, while Leonardo's works are still alive and understood, the music of his contemporaries, though of incomparable artistry, is a closed book to most musicians. Even composers who lived and created two hundred years later than that, must be exhumed by the musicologist and their scores handed over to the performing artists with copious commentary and instructions.

The essential problems of music in eighteenth-century England were, first of all, the degree of imaginative freedom that could be reconciled with the strong prejudices against the reigning musical style coming from Italy; secondly, whether restraint upon the power of imagination can produce what we ordinarily understand by a work of art; and, thirdly, whether the ends that were being pursued were in fact creative ends, whether they lent themselves to great art as well as to great national enterprise.

Most foreign historians, and not a few of the British, have considered eighteenth-century England a musical wasteland, or, as the Germans contemptuously used to refer to it, *Das Land ohne Musik*. Even so perceptive a connoisseur of eighteenth-century music as Romain Rolland (who began his career as a knowledgable musicologist) sadly stated that, when Handel arrived in England in 1710, the art of music was dead in the land of his choice.[1] It does seem, when we look at the meagre publications of English music available from this period, that English composers each day took their docile muse out of her stall, gave her a few carrots, then climbed on her back, letting her go whither she would. An air of musical mediocrity seems to envelop the islands.

On the English side, many writers are agreed that what snuffed out native music in England was the overwhelming figure of the Saxon immigrant, Handel, who virtually prevented the emergence of native music. The finality of these opinions, with the lack of knowledge of eighteenth-century music—and of Handel himself—has made it very difficult for the modern scholar to find the cracks through which to penetrate the wall of ignorance and misrepresentation, especially since Handel's strong influence on English music is an indisputable fact. For a hundred years after Handel's death he dominated English musical thought, as Wagner did German. *Messiah* became part of the Englishman's religion, and he would no more find fault with this music than he would with the words of the Bible, and this in spite of the distortion of this famous score by arrangers and performers. But then, since Handel did become a national symbol, his music on the lips of every Englishman, why did he not initiate a national school as did Lully, another immigrant, in France? Obviously there must have been many other forces at work to create this unique situation, for the scene blotted out by Handel's heroic figure is vivid with a jostling crowd of men and ideas, and there was in England a priceless musical heritage.

England entered the seventeenth century with a rich and highly developed vocal and instrumental literature, some of it well in advance of the Continent. The musical references and scenes in Shakespeare alone are a convincing testimonial to the universal love of music in all walks of English life, and there was a wealth of engaging folk music. Literary scholars know about the influence of wandering English theatrical troupes in the north of Germany and in the Scandinavian countries; it is less well known that musicians accompanied or followed these troupes, disseminating English music on the Continent. Many of these musicians remained there, exerting considerable influence on European music. To mention one example, William Brade, a fine violist and composer, finally settled in Hamburg in the 1620s as head of municipal music. His influence on the German dance suite can be followed virtually to the time of Bach.[1] Up to this time English music was a European phenomenon, however modified by local conditions, but by the middle of the century local factors become dominant, not simply influencing the course of music but forming its actual shape. The forces at work were numerous and interacting. Geographical discovery and colonialism worked powerfully on men's minds, the removal of old checks gave impetus to individual ambitions, and the English Reformation, with all its infinite consequences for music, entered upon a new phase. All this caused a woeful artistic letdown that is usually explained simply by the hostility of the Commonwealth and of the Puritan mind to music. But the Commonwealth cannot be held responsible for the eclipse of music beyond a certain degree.[1] Puritans, especially Cromwell's army, did destroy musical instruments, hacked church organs to pieces, and burned musical scores; furthermore they did banish music from the church services and dispersed the fine cathedral choirs, certainly a serious loss. But all this was done for very special reasons. The Puritan hostility to music in the Church stemmed from the indelible association in the non-conformist mind of the arts with the service of the old church, of Catholicism. It was thus in all Protestant lands except in Lutheran Germany. Luther's Teutonic romantic emotions and his bois-terous tongue came in music to disciplined issue, laying the foundations for an incomparable school of music, culminating in Bach. Calvin's methodical and uncompromising mind refused accommodation with the past, and, wherever his sway held, music simply shrivelled, in many places to nothingness. In his private life the English Puritan did not frown on music; Cromwell himself was as fond of it as any Stuart king, and Milton, a musician's son, loved music as much as did Shakespeare. It was during the Commonwealth that public musical entertainment for a paying audience was introduced, a socio-artistic innovation of far-reaching consequences. There were many foreign musicians in London who made a good living and there was a flourishing music-printing industry. John Playford's *Introduction to the Skill of Music* was published in 1655, to become for half a century the most important didactic manual. Such publications even contained lists of reputable music teachers. Yet something essential was missing in this lively musical practice: real creative fervour and ability. The reason for this void—and here the Commonwealth must bear the blame—was that at this crucial period in musical history, when every thread led to the theatre, to opera, the English theatres were closed. The principal musical idiom of the century—and of the next one—which ever since Monteverdi was the main source for musical techniques and expressive means, was rejected, and the English composer, like the Swiss or the Dutch, who also balked at this Italian 'invention', had nowhere to go.

With the Restoration the old religious motives ceased to operate, and a strong wave of refreshing Italian and French influence seems to have roused English music from complacency and conformity. The Chapel Royal, hitherto the focal point of English musical life, was re-established, Charles created a court orchestra on the pattern of Louis XIV's, the cathedral choirs were reinstated, and the reopened theatres immediately responded to music. A specifically English genre was now cultivated, the ode or welcome song, a sort of secular cantata, and the anthem was also enriched with the addition of the orchestra.[1] The elements of this music, aside from the chorus, were of operatic origin (as they were of course in Bach's Passions) and even a good deal of the choral style came from the English theatre, rather than from the choir loft of the church. It was at this juncture that Handel arrived in England, and it did not take him long to discover that the services at St Paul's Cathedral were totally different from those in Our Lady's Lutheran church in Halle. The economic motive had penetrated deeply into both politics and religion, leading to a close alliance of the two. The ringing anthems and Te Deums Handel heard, and later composed, were not so much acts of worship as dynastic–national celebrations at which the Lord was informed about the Englishman's latest deeds and requested to ratify foregone conclusions. Although set to Old Testament texts, there was no essential difference between one of these anthems and a birthday ode for the king; both were purely ceremonial music. Following Purcell's magnificent example, the German immigrant gave his new compatriots the *Utrecht* and *Dettingen Te Deums*, the Chandos and the Coronation Anthems, works that surpassed anything ever heard in this category. The grandeur and the almost graphic theatricality of this wonderful music made every Englishman absolutely convinced that his elected constitutional God,

Jehovah, would support him in his righteous enterprises. I say 'every Englishman', because the Nonconformists also came to these services; they were regarded as state functions. However, our central problem concerns opera, not Anglican church music, and, before reaching any conclusions about the mysterious decline of music in eighteenth-century England, we must examine this puzzling phenomenon called opera.

We often take for granted the existence of a natural, as distinguished from a cultivated, taste for music. This predisposition by affinity is quite enough to explain why the Italian people are as ardent and direct toward opera as others are to a field of daffodils. It would seem natural, therefore, that, since this musical taste differs vastly from the English, it would be extremely difficult for English musicians to feel at home in it. Still, English musicians did respond to the spirit of this new art that in the meantime had conquered all of Europe; that they did not succeed in creating their own opera is another matter we shall presently discuss.

It is curious how little attention has been paid by historians to this presence of the new musical idiom, although musicians of the period felt it instinctively. Indeed, in the many plays with music the language and idiom of opera gradually took hold, and by the end of the seventeenth century England had produced Purcell, one of the great musico-dramatic talents in history. But in all these so-called 'English' or 'semi'-operas the participants are clearly differentiated into actors, singers, and dancers; the essential operatic structure was missing. Purcell had a keen appreciation of the psycho-physical tides of 'atmosphere' and of the cores of personality between which they ebb and flow. He failed, however, to exploit or elaborate these perceptions beyond exquisite individual songs or scenes; in fact, he deliberately held himself within certain limits, because what the critics called a play 'all sung' was unacceptable to Englishmen. Opera seemed to them a

mere succession of unnatural oddities, of expressive figures unexpected and illogical in their moves, an example of insensibility
to refinement. That its music can be beautiful was generally
conceded, but what kind of theatre is this where instead of speaking
intelligibly the actors sing?[1]

If examined as a dramatic genre, we see in fact that the very
criteria which make for great literary drama declare war on opera.
When opera endeavours to emulate the spoken drama by being
compact and swift, those qualities are opposed by another element
that constantly upsets the theatrical continuity and seemingly
destroys it—lyricism. Dramatic concentration, the fast dialogue,
the motion, the liveliness are all masks; the spirit that animates
them is not drama but lyricism. The dialogue is condensed
precisely to make room for lyricism; the action is swift only to be
completely arrested by lyric effusion. The action and events in an
opera do not unfold in an orderly and logical fashion; they either
rush head over heel or are suspended. And in that unique and most
characteristic possession of opera, the ensemble, in which several
figures express their innermost thoughts simultaneously, the text
can be apprehended only in snippets. The tempo of the spoken
drama also fluctuates; lyricism is present there too, but everything
issues naturally from plot and action; the lyric moments are not
primary; the action is not conducted for their sake. But in opera
the lyric moments are primary and this constitutes the basic
difference between opera and drama.

We cannot simply let the question rest at the statement that
opera is a paradox; we still have to explain why most great
musicians were so irresistibly attracted to it and why in England it
was rejected until recent times. Actually, it was opera's very
paradoxical nature that assured its triumph.

Drama projects a chapter from life in a more or less stylised
form. Stylised representation has degrees, it is exponential; we
increase the stylisation, square it, when we use certain devices like
verse. But, even though highly stylised, a play in verse still presents

a degree of realism. The play becomes an opera if the stylisation is cubed, indeed carried *ad absurdum*, when all the figures in the drama sing. And who could dispute that the primacy of song is natural in a genre that is sung from beginning to end? Yet, because music expresses dramatically decisive feelings with more intensity than words, the dramatic effect of dramatic situations is infinitely enhanced. In a word, operatic conventions are not necessarily anti-dramatic, but they are anti-literary. We may say that in opera the most dramatic drama and the most lyric lyricism alternate, and this wavelike process can be followed down to the single arias and recitatives. No other genre unites lyricism and drama with such intensity and in such opposite yet compatible fashion. This is opera's aesthetic justification; it is this that made even the arch-symphonist Beethoven prostrate himself before the Janus face of opera.

The key to the aesthetic significance of opera, then, is that the emotional nuances of a stylised interpretation of life, the intensity of feelings, the inner dramatic elements of the human soul, are most overwhelmingly caught by music: drama necessarily begets music from its own womb. It is in this natural process that opera was conceived. The young Nietzsche's enthusiastically advanced theory of the birth of tragedy from the spirit of music is valid for antiquity and the Middle Ages, but by the late sixteenth century it is no longer applicable. True, they did sing in Shakespeare's plays, but the plays themselves owe nothing to music; the modern theatre in England and Spain is a new genre whose origins do not go back to music or to religious rites and whose principles are independently their own. These were the very countries, England and Spain, the originators of the modern theatre, which failed to produce native opera, both of them preferring a compromise lyric theatre in which music was an accessory rather than a principal force. It is here that the riddle of English music in the eighteenth century must be sought, for a glance at the map of eighteenth-century music will show a meagre spoken theatre and an overflowing abundance of opera in Italy, opposed to a flourishing stage in England to the exclusion of native opera.[1] In eighteenth-century Italy, all branches of literature took second place to opera, or, if not, contributed to its wide acceptance, whereas in England everything seems to have conspired to prevent the rise of a true lyric theatre. This was the age of wit and intellect. The English were accustomed in their spoken theatre to logical procedures, witty dialogues, and intelligible plots. They correctly felt that music added to the words, rather than being subordinate, is capable of absorbing them. And, of course, in an opera the dimensions of each are completely changed because, as we have said, lyricism is the primary force. It is a primacy that a highly developed theatrical culture will not accept without protest. This is one of the two keys to the entire subsequent history of music in England up to the end of the nineteenth century when the great revival set in; if it is not understood we are far off the mark. The literary world in England declared war on opera, particularly Italian opera. Pope called it a 'harlot form' (*Dunciad*), and Johnson found the classic stricture when he said that opera is 'an exotick and irrational entertainment' (*Lives of the Poets*). But this curious antipathy remained alive practically to our own day. As recently as 1935, Sir Walford Davies, then Master of the King's Music, thought that opera 'seems still an astonishing and phenomenal enormity'.

This, then, is the situation: opera, although it is the core of well over two centuries of musical thought, was consistently derided and belittled in the English-speaking world. Since the spirit, idiom, and technique of opera directly or indirectly determined most music of the seventeenth and eighteenth centuries, English music dropped out of the mainstream of Western music. Only once did English musico-dramatic genius flare up in fullness of stature, in Purcell, but he died tragically young, and even he trespassed the limits of English musical dramaturgy only once, in a magnificent miniature opera, *Dido and Aeneas*, which, significantly, was composed for a young ladies' school and not for the public theatre.

At this point let us look for the other key to the riddle of eighteenth-century English music, just at the time when that mighty figure of a man, Handel, arrived in England. For two centuries the world has been accustomed to see in the creator of *Messiah* the 'composer in ordinary to the Protestant religion', a man who abandoned the frivolities of opera to devote the rest of his life to the exaltation of Holy Writ. But this Saxon was not a religious composer; he was a conqueror, an artistic gambler, an impresario, as well as one of the greatest musicians the world has known. He came to England after having conquered the Italians at their own game in their own land, and now he wanted to carve an empire for himself in English musical life. Eventually he succeeded, becoming the English national composer *par excellence*, but his path was tortuous and full of trials, his initial success notwithstanding. When he arrived in England his main concern was Italian opera, which he composed for the select circle of the nobility, meeting with occasional triumph and frequent rejection. Meanwhile, with his phenomenal ability to absorb different styles, he soon espied the particular English tone in Purcell's and other English composers' music and was able to plunge into their world with his first 'English' works, the *Birthday Ode for Queen Anne*, and the *Utrecht Te Deum* (1713). The anthems were also English and Anglican to the core, without the slightest resemblance to the Lutheran music in which he was trained in his youth. Similarly, his pastorals exhaled the unmistakable spirit of the English countryside. Still, what was uppermost in his mind was Italian opera and he was unwilling to abandon it. Either he was slow in recognising the innate English opposition to opera, especially Italian opera, or he believed that he could overcome it. The struggle was gigantic, and was complicated by politics, because the Tories used the German musician as a tool in their opposition to the German king. The London public liked Handel and always stood by in crises, but their dislike of the Hanoverian dynasty was strong, and the German king's favourite German musician was a convenient means both for an indirect attack on the House of Hanover and a more direct weapon to be used on those who supported it, like Robert Walpole. The war was fought savagely, in pamphlets and cartoons and satires; nor were Handel's opponents above hiring thugs to beat up his audiences so as to scare them away from the theatre, all the while hoping that a defeat for the German composer would reflect adversely on the king himself. Worst of all, the literary leaders, headed by Horace Walpole and Swift, joined his enemies because they felt that Italian opera injected an undesirable, destructive, and alien element in English tradition. Three times circumstances defeated Handel's operatic enterprise, though the stories about his bankruptcies are inaccurate; he was too shrewd a businessman not to know when to cut his losses. But after each débâcle he came back, and some of his operas had tremendous successes. Presently he began to take stock. He noticed that his English works were far more popular than the Italian operas and permitted him more freedom of action than the Venetian–Neapolitan type of opera. The rigorous principles of the *opera seria* increasingly limited him. In the last operas he searched earnestly for a way out, and there is an exquisite new tone, an intimate and highly sophisticated humour that was totally lost on his contemporaries, even on Charles Burney, a great admirer of the composer, and is still little appreciated by us. At any rate, by about 1740 Handel realised that he needed space and freedom in which to develop his powers, and for this the oratorio, planned on the pattern of the Greek drama, that is, with the active participation of the chorus, was the answer. For generations we have been told that Handel's change from opera to oratorio was the result of a religious conversion and that these works are the epitome of sacred music, but this was a later and false interpretation. The oratorio, or more precisely the English music drama, was an entirely personal creation of this naturalised Briton and had nothing to do with the Italian prototype by that name. Nor had it any connections with the German oratorio-Passion, as the Germans would have it, and the bracketing of Handel's name with Bach's is altogether unjustified.

Handel, with his sharp sense of observation, realised that he could continue to write dramatic music only by placing his opera in a framework suitable to English tastes. He was not attracted to pietism in any of its forms; he was not a mystic like Bach; he was a dramatist, and what interested him exclusively were people whom he could manipulate dramatically, not articles of faith. Yet the one oratorio he wrote on New Testament verses, *Messiah*, which was a commission from the Dublin Charities Association, became the norm by which posterity has judged him, and this despite the two dozen other great works composed on English texts, none of which had a Christian-religious content. This distorted view of both the composer and his work is the reverse of contemporary eighteenth-century opinion. The oratorio was then suspected to be camouflaged opera, which in many ways it was, and in the case of such works as *Semele* or *Hercules* it was indeed true English opera. The oratorio, even *Messiah*, was called a 'polite and elegant entertainment', and in ecclesiastical circles and among many of the public this trifling with the Word of God was viewed with alarm and distaste. The interdiction of staged performances by the bishop of London compelled concert presentations of essentially stage works, and thus arose the 'oratorio manner'. The original stage directions, plainly evident in the manuscript scores, were deleted in the printed editions early in the nineteenth century. But the public responded to many of the oratorios and to their passionate flesh-and-blood heroes, Samson, Joshua, Saul, and all the others, whom they already knew well from their Bible, and with whom they found it natural to identify themselves. They also liked the pastorals, but the great classical dramas as well as the last introspective oratorios that did not have the rousing anthem-like choruses extolling Jehovah's power in trumpeting Hallelujahs were total failures. By the end of his life, Handel had become a national institution, and was buried among the great in Westminster Abbey.

Then began the great mystification. The Handelian oratorio, which came from and was destined for the theatre, was viewed as coming from the choir loft. Opera being avoided, the only large-scale vocal music remaining was of a 'sacred' nature, and, since for the mass of the people mythology is nine-tenths of religion, it was easy to imagine these music dramas on biblical subjects to be sacred music. The legend of Handel as the great Christian composer started soon after his death, but reached its full proportions in the nineteenth century, when his scores were published in popular editions. The many ardent and poetical love scenes were excised or modified to guard the Victorian image of the great religious composer. At the same time the worship of this plaster image of the sainted musician became so pervasive that Handel did indeed become the unwitting force that stifled English music. Oratorios were composed by the hundreds all the way to the end of the nineteenth century, as were anthems of all descriptions, and such derivative and commonplace music became the chief concern of both composers and public. Except for the embarrassing passages, practically every other page of the Old Testament was set to music either in the original or in atrocious 'poetic' paraphrases. And, when that was not enough, the works of the great continental composers, Mozart, Haydn, and others, fitted with biblical texts, were converted into pious *contrafacta*. It is interesting that almost all these oratorios, as well as the anthems, were based on the Old Testament, while Lutheran Germany was partial in the cantata (and of course in the settings of the Passion) to the New Testament. But, while to Handel the figures of Hebrew folklore and history were living human beings, to these composers, inhibited by an *a priori* religious attitude, they appeared as marble busts. They could not comfortably manage the formally majestic, and the oratorio became a manner turned into a formula, 'stucco made to look like stone'. The same fate overtook the anthem, so splendid in Purcell's and Handel's hands. Englishmen like ritual if it be dignified and decorous, and the typical eighteenth-century Englishman looked at religious services as a harmless and even praiseworthy provider of a form of spiritual entertainment. The churches resounded to perfunctory Hallelujah choruses that became quasi-obligatory after Handel; but where was the magnificent *élan* of Handel's Coronation Anthems or the wondrous pastoral intimacy of some of the Chandos Anthems? The unsleeping sense of dramatic effect that characterises both the Handelian oratorio and anthem was replaced by watery sentimentalism and unadventurous paper music.

This lamentable state of affairs was worsened by the system of higher education in music, which in England centred around the universities. On the Continent a musician was apprenticed to a master and thus was kept within the living mainstream of music. In England, as in latter-day America, where this unique system was inherited and followed with a vengeance, he was subjected to music study that consisted in imitating the techniques of the great composers of the past, that is, textbook music. They were mastering the craft, not the art, of composition. For a century after Handel's death they were instructed in a pseudo-Handelian style, writing innumerable anthems, oratorios, and organ pieces in 'correct' style, a procedure that guaranteed sterility. Correctness, easy accessibility, and avoidance of any personal imagination were considered the artistic virtues. Essays and criticisms about these works, from the eighteenth to the early twentieth century, abound in such compliments as 'the work of a musician and a gentleman', or 'this music is clean and healthy', or 'mercifully free of theatrical emptiness'. The public itself, though fond of music, wanted to be entertained and nothing more.

Nevertheless, eighteenth-century musical life in England, though the figure of Handel blotted it from us, was anything but bleak and arid as is commonly believed even by Englishmen. With the influx of Italian singers and composers as well as French and German musicians, a solid core of able professionals took its place in London's musical life, and by the opening of the Handelian era a respectable number of knowledgeable amateurs joined their ranks. The commercial aspects of music also received considerable attention, London being one of the greatest centres for music publishing, rivalling Amsterdam and Paris not only in quality and quantity, but also in the fine art of piracy. The new pianoforte was enthusiastically taken over and for almost a century English pianos were the best instruments available. Beethoven still treasured his piano made by Broadwood. The level of performance was high. Handel's performances at the Haymarket Theatre were praised not only by the local worthies, but by all visiting maestros, among them Quantz and Gluck, both exacting performers used to excellent ensembles. In the 1760s the King's Band was a fine modern orchestra which with the superbly trained choir of the Chapel Royal could cope with anything the age's musical literature offered.[1] A whole array of distinguished foreign musicians came to England, some of them settling there permanently; indeed, the list is a veritable who's who of eighteenth-century music: Handel, Geminiani, Bononcini, Loeillet, Ariosti, Galuppi, John Christian Bach, Abel, Haydn, Clementi, and so forth. The provinces, too, began to foster their own musical life, and concert societies were established in Bath, Manchester, Salisbury, as well as Dublin, where *Messiah* was first performed. It was in England that festivals were first organised; the famous Three Choirs Festival started as early as 1724, that is, far ahead of such events on the Continent. Nor was the intellectual and literary side of music neglected. England initiated modern musical historiography with Burney and Hawkins, modern musical aesthetics with Webb and Avison, and the Academy of Ancient Music was, *mutatis mutandis*, the first musicological institute in the world.[2]

We have seen that eighteenth-century London was one of the

musical capitals in the West—but we have not yet said anything about native English composers. Here again the misapplied Handel worship is to be blamed, for the musical world simply does not know this music, deprecated by the English themselves. Greene, Boyce, Battishill, Croft, the two Wesleys, Linley, Dibdin, and many others are little more than names, yet they would hold their own in very good musical company. Anyone who examines the manuscripts of Boyce's royal odes in the Bodleian will see fine and imaginative music, yet it is still unpublished. As to Thomas Augustine Arne, there was an original British talent from whom even Handel learned a good deal.[1]

The eighteenth century produced two new genres that were thoroughly English: the glee and the ballad opera. Though eventually the glees declined into mere doggerel, there were many fine compositions in this large literature which is still not sufficiently explored. As to the ballad opera, aside from the fact that it was one of the ancestors of the German *Singspiel* that led to *The Magic Flute*, it offers an important additional clue to the working of the English musical mind in the eighteenth century.[2] Though Burke called the *Beggar's Opera* subversive in social tendency, and Johnson saw in it principles injurious to morality, the important fact is that this highly original creation is the prototype of the modern musical comedy; not of comic opera or operetta, but of comedy with music. Triumphal arches do not go well with humour, and the English, thwarted by the frosty majesty of the *opera seria*, reached back into their very own theatrical *savoir faire*. But once more care is indicated when assaying this new genre. There is nothing original about this ballad opera—except its text and construction, that is, the purely theatrical element. The music consisted of a medley of old and well-known popular tunes and, significantly, of borrowed and parodied opera numbers, mostly from Handel, all of it merely arranged by Pepusch in the simplest manner. We do not even have a full score of the original —if one ever existed—only the tunes. But as a theatrical production the *Beggar's Opera* is still fresh and viable, long after it caused the most spectacular defeat for Handel and Italian opera. Ballads and popular songs can throw more light on a people's outlook and temperament than the content of archives. Composers did write oratorios, even some operas, but in these fields they lacked the conviction and the creative genius to fashion living characters in music. They could add music, however, to a good play with living characters.

This then is an abbreviated sketch of the music of an age that teemed with activity, but also with prejudice and aprioristic attitudes. We are still awaiting a musical Sir Leslie Stephen or Allardyce Nicoll to write its history.

CHAPTER 6

THE WRITER

by Bertrand H. Bronson

If we ponder the matter, we are likely to conclude that literary art, had it not already arisen, could hardly have got started in a world where printing was an available medium. Literature is so deeply rooted in the oral, beneath the written, stratum that, when we write, our traditional choices of phrase are conditioned by the primordial instinct. The signs are in the language itself: we 'speak the tongue that Shakespeare spake', 'It is well *said* by a noted *writer*'.[1] Literature is so naturally, so fundamentally, an affair of *telling*, as opposed to *recording*, that the traces are omnipresent:

> But first I pray yow, of your curteisye,
> That ye n'arette it nat my vileynye,
> Thogh that I pleynly *speke* in this mateere,
> To *telle* yow hir wordes and hir cheere,
> Ne thogh I *speke* hir wordes proprely...
> Whoso shal *telle* a *tale* after a man,
> He moot reherce as ny as evere he kan
> Everich a word.[2]

Or, in the nineteenth century, at random,

> To know the change and feel it,
> When there is none to heal it,
> Nor numbèd sense to steel it,
>   Was never *said* in rhyme.[3]

If this seem a trivial point, it is important to correct the impression. For the relation of author and public, actual or imagined, expressed or implied, is of profound significance to literary causes and effects, a universally pervasive concern of the subtlest psycho-

logical complexity and abiding perplexity. The gradual detachment, through print, of the writer from a present and familiar
audience is one of the most far-reaching influences of modern
times in our western civilisation; and its special problems emerge
with crucial insistence for the first time in the eighteenth century.
Not that the question was simple, even before the invention of
printing: but it was different.

Chaucer's example is useful at the outset. He was the gifted
inheritor of an *oral* tradition a millennium old, but sophisticated
by careful study of the Romans and improved by genius for its
own immediate purposes. How subtle an instrument it became in
his hands is only of late coming to be recognised, critically discussed and disputed, in the light—or shadow—of subsequent
experimentation with narrative techniques. Tales like those of the
Wife of Bath, the Merchant, or the Nun's Priest, in which
characters speaking in their individual ways are presented by other
characters with their own personal bias, who in turn are quoted by
a narrator who is the posed and highlighted self-portrait of the
poet who, himself visible and audible, projects these inventions
with histrionic skill upon the senses of a present audience: such
tales are a study in mental refraction sufficiently complex. But the
overriding fact in this complexity is the original rapport between
Chaucer and his hearers. Many of these were his personal friends
and most of them he probably knew by sight. He wrote with their
outlook in mind, with the conditions of a personal oral delivery
in mind. This familiarity, abetted at need by tone of voice, by a
look, and ever checked by the involuntary, spontaneous response
of attention intimately observed, made for him the effective ambit
of creative possibility beyond which he did not need, or perhaps
wish, to venture. That he must have thought of being read in
other places and later times does not affect his creative technique
in the least. Human nature changes at a geological rate, and, if
Virgil and Ovid can speak to *us*, shall we not be understood by
those that come after? *The Hous of Fame* and the epilogue to

Troilus and Criseyde are a sufficient commentary on that question as it concerned Chaucer. The present point is how very manifest are the influences of the *social conditions* within which he works, how enormous their benefits, how confidently he seizes advantages made available by them, how sensitively he perceives the opportunities and limitations of these quasi-personal relations, so that we vicariously seem to know him better than we know our next-door neighbour.

Thus much space has been accorded to Chaucer because he can stand as the ideal paradigm of a kind of relationship between poet and audience that existed for centuries. Nor, of course, though printing would eventually transform it, did the situation change immediately or suddenly with the invention of printing. In the sphere with which we are at the moment concerned, the effect on contemporary thought and practice was slight. Poems circulated in manuscript copies, primarily among friends and acquaintances, and were doubtless read aloud to small interested groups, in upper-class society. Ambitious and aspiring works were written with such an audience in view. Lyrics and private effusions were written for private presentation or to be sung; sometimes for particular occasions. Poets had no other kind of publication in mind, and hardly envisaged any other kind of reader. Why should anything so personal be printed? Publication by print came in time to be recognised as a safeguard against corruption by miscopying, and as a kind of insurance against loss; but was not resorted to by the author himself without apology and at least the pretence of his having been driven to publishing in self-protection, for the integrity of his work. Not financial protection; for what mercenary reward worth considering could a poet hope for or expect? A *dedicated* work might attract a present, large or small, but publication had nothing to do with such a gift. When Queen Elizabeth ordered Burleigh to reward Spenser with £100, he protested, 'What! all this for a song?' Spenser, at any rate, anticipated no commercial profit from the *sale* of his work, nor in fact was there any system or convention to ensure payment. His audience was an enlightened circle of connoisseurs. *A fortiori*, Shakespeare's sonnets were not matter for a printer, and doubtless were issued without the author's knowledge or consent. As for the plays—and as for drama generally—they were made for living performance and subject to continual alteration according to changing circumstances and current theatrical need. Publication was simply irrelevant. Drama was an *oral* art. Play-*printing* was an art of embalming. Time enough, after a playwright's death, to think of collecting and printing his works. While he lived, they were worth more to him on the stage than on the shelf. On the shelf, in fact, they might be a palpable disadvantage, profitable only to thieves.

Shakespeare and his fellow-playwrights always had a cross-section of their total contemporary—if not potential—audience in full and present view, just as Chaucer had had. They could study their reactions and cut the cloth to suit the emergent taste. They could show them their own image, analyse their form and body, and interpret them to themselves. The gamut was wider than Chaucer's, more democratic, but the connection between author and audience was close and capable of accurate tuning all along the scale. There need be little uncertainty in the dramatist's mind as to whether his work was reverberating with the intended resonance.

Poetry and drama flourished in the Elizabethan age without asking help from printing, and apart from poetry and drama imaginative literature as yet was small in amount and of slight importance. Printing was not only inessential to the life of poetry but even a rude encroachment upon its aristocratic preserves and oral traditions. By and large, printing was still an irresponsible upstart and intruder, regarded with jealous suspicion by literary society and by the State. The number of presses was arbitrarily limited and their output restricted in various ways under both Tudors and Stuarts. The medium continued to be relatively un-respectable in the world of *belles lettres* for at least a hundred years longer—a fact that can be detected in the reluctance of authors, so late as past the mid-eighteenth century, to admit their names to the title-pages of their published work. For women, of course, the indecency lasted for still another century.

Certainly until after the Civil Wars literature was the leisured accomplishment of amateurs—authors without a professional compulsion, not writing for a livelihood, and under no sort of commitment to the press. The war spawned a great deal of controversial publication, both political and religious, but not yet literary. This ephemeral writing, however, as it became more frequent, also began to develop habits of greater regularity, so that by means of journals and periodicals a new kind of outlet for literary expression appeared, to be exploited in the next age. What appeared in these media of belletristic writing, like essays, tales, brief biographies, may be considered the first generation of literature conceived and conditioned by its commercial purpose and mode of existence. As such, it constitutes a turning-point of vast consequence in the relations between author and audience. From this moment onwards, gradually but increasingly, there develops a race of authors who write to an indefinite body of readers, personally undifferentiated and unknown; who accept this separation as a primary condition of their creative activity and address their public invisibly, through the curtain, opaque and impersonal, of print: writers to whom in due course, as J. W. Saunders puts it, 'print became the normal, and in time entirely respectable, medium of communication with any audience, and prose the normal language of professional literary expression'.[1] The questions raised by this altered relationship, the variety of ways in which a solution has been attempted, are intertwined with most of the significant literary problems that have arisen in the last two and a half centuries, and have never been more troublesome and disturbing than they are today.

The Writer

2

Changes so profound did not proceed at an equal pace in all branches of literature. Poetry, though it had in the end to accept and live with the new conditions of dissemination, could afford to be more resistant to these influences. Especially in its higher reaches, it had a very ancient and well-understood tradition that sustained its patrician estate and kept it conservative in hereditary sur-roundings, and aloof from the chaffering world of prose. Its appeal was to a culture and a kind of audience long familiar. So long as it could find a means of support free of commercial conditions, it was relatively secure. It did not have to modify its address or recognise an altered relationship on account of publi-cation in print.

The reading public of Milton, Cowley, Waller, Dryden, Prior —and even, to a degree, thanks to the unique confluence of genius and character, of Pope himself—was probably roughly commen-surate with their social world as a whole. We have only to read over the list of subscribers to Prior's great folio of 1718, *Poems on Several Occasions*—the title-page does not carry its author's name —to see that this is true. Dedicatory letters frequently confirm the fact. We must, however, recognise that subscription publication was in itself a sign of change, and a necessary concession to the weakening of aristocratic obligations under the old system of support. But lofty poetry was, as Saunders has remarked, 'in-dispensable to Augustanism'. It occupies the status of 'the civilising literary art par excellence'.[1] It is at once the proof, and the measure, of high value in that cultural ideal, and this of course is why it was of such importance that Pope or another should crown the age with an epic—just as, upholding the classical values later in the century, Reynolds and his followers aspired to paint 'heroic' subjects in the grand manner of Michelangelo: epics of the sister art.

But, on a less exalted plane, it is worth contemplating briefly the advantages which so distinguished an artist as Prior could derive from his sympathetic and intimate rapport with that select audience of his. The differences of Church and State between them were far less considerable to his art than the community of education, the common circle of acquaintance at the university and in town, the same reading, a shared vocabulary, similar experiences, *like* amusements and games, a kindred range of allusion, clichés, tricks of phrase, speech cadences on a common tonic. Such a community knows all the by-ways and short-cuts of conversational interchange as well as a schoolboy knows his physical surroundings; and an art that can employ this intimacy of reference can convey abundant meaning, on subjects proper to it, with the greatest verbal economy. The artist—say Prior— knows that six-sevenths of his poetic substance can be safely lodged, and to better effect, in his reader's imagination if only he select the right seventh to show. It is an art wherein, to change the figure, the harmonics are more important than the fundamental notes. But, continuing the musical analogy, we know that you cannot elicit the same timbre from every sort of instrument. Prior is an exquisite composer for the instrument he knows best—his own public. He is as sensitive to its overtones as Chopin to those of the piano. His most refined effects are calculated for it alone, and indeed are things unattemptable and inconceivable elsewhere:

> She, first of all the Town, was told,
> Where newest INDIA Things were sold:
> So in a Morning, without Bodice,
> Slipt sometimes out to Mrs. THODY's;
> To cheapen Tea, to buy a Screen:
> What else cou'd so much Virtue mean?
> For to prevent the least Reproach,
> BETTY went with Her in the Coach.
>
> But when no very great Affair
> Excited her peculiar Care;
> She without fail was wak'd at Ten;

Drank Chocolate, then slept again:
At Twelve She rose: with much ado
Her Cloaths were huddl'd on by Two:
Then; Does my Lady Dine at home?
Yes sure;—but is the Colonel come?
Next, how to spend the Afternoon,
And not come Home again too soon;
The Change, the City, or the Play,
As each was proper for the Day;
A Turn in Summer to HYDE-PARK,
When it grew tolerably Dark.[1]

Prior was almost the last considerable poet with opportunities of this kind to prompt and condition his art.

At the higher reaches the problem is not acute. There are time-honoured ways of beginning—which is the chief embarrassment, as Johnson observes in his first *Rambler* paper. The hieratic robes are in themselves a cloak, and the god-inspired poet is not supposed to appear in the glare of day. He is rather to be heard than seen, whether he invoke the Muses or an honoured name:

Descend, ye Nine! descend and sing![2]

or

Awake, my St. John! leave all meaner things
To low ambition, and the pride of Kings.[3]

But, as patronage ebbed and the tide of print rose, the serious poet faced a serious problem. If he knew how to address a 'fit audience though few', that audience would hardly support him. If he was to live, he had to find place and preferment. For a brief time, this was not too difficult for literary merit to do. The great Whig and Tory statesmen made it their business to look out for most of the abler writers in the days of Anne. The posts these writers found were supposed to leave them leisure to write; but on the other hand there were conditions and consequences. Their status as poets necessarily became more amateur, while they devoted time and energy to political activity, whether in office or by the pen. Prose was here far more effective than poetry, and for these men prose became a duty. Indeed, the obligations of office could almost remove them from the sphere of *belles lettres*. Steele became more interested in politics than letters. Addison managed to evolve a compromise reasonably suited to his gifts. Swift never laid claim to being a literary man: published anonymously or not at all, and certainly always from unmercenary and unprofessional motives. Prior was an able but reluctant diplomatist who would have preferred a life of poetry. Gay never found a satisfactory solution, and for all his gifts and occasional successes, remained a frustrated poet.

Of all the Augustans of Anne's and the first George's day, Pope was the only avowed, lifelong, wholly dedicated poet. There was never, among his varied interests, any question of the primacy of poetry:

> This subtle Thief of life, this paltry Time,
> What will it leave me, if it snatch my rhyme?
> If ev'ry wheel of that unweary'd Mill,
> That turn'd ten thousand verses, now stands still?[1]

Goldsmith might look back with nostalgia to the days 'when the great Somers was at the helm' as the golden age of patronage, but it was only relatively so, and in fact Pope derived none but indirect benefits from the current posture of affairs. Poetry was not a dependable calling, even so early; and it very much concerns us to study the means Pope devised to make it approximately so for himself, in the face of his special handicaps of ill health and a religion whereby he was 'deny'd all posts of profit and of trust'.

Initially, of course, we grant him modest means, determination, self-command, and the genius to win recognition early in life. Next, since patronage did not seek him out, he compelled a kind of dispersed and shared patronage by subscription. By his subscribers he was at once sustained and supplied with a primary audience that constituted a surrogate for that earlier traditional, aural–oral relation and a partial escape from the facelessness of an anonymous public. Next, he singled out from the larger body of his supporting audience various particular friends in order to address them by name in his Horatian imitations, and of these moral essays, epistles, or satires he made a more and more personal thing, turning the discourse into some semblance of dialogue, and sprinkling the text with familiar allusion to contemporaries. To these, in spite of their intimate, conversational tone, he gave such extreme finish that they derogate very little from his claim to be regarded as a poet of the very highest order. But, at the same time, they rescued him from the frustrating sense of bardic isolation, from the fate ironically hit off in the epistle already quoted:

> Go, lofty Poet! and in such a crowd,
> Sing thy sonorous verse—but not aloud!—[1]

a fate altogether likely in a patronless world of print, *sans* visible audience.

A further move in the same direction of projecting the image of a select Augustan community within which he lived and fraternised, was to contrive the publication of his literary correspondence. This was tantamount to a prose translation of the verse epistles— more informal, with the added charm of apparent actuality: a kind of eavesdropping on the best company. What a revelation! and how reassuring to any doubters of Pope's assumed rights of superiority, as adumbrated in his scornful verses:

> Ask you what Provocation I have had?
> The strong Antipathy of Good to Bad.
> When Truth or Virtue an Affront endures,
> Th'Affront is mine, my friend, and should be yours...
> Yes, I am proud; I must be proud to see
> Men not afraid of God, afraid of me...[2]

In these ways, and by such means, Pope was in actual fact creating his chosen audience in his own ideal image, recovering from the alien world of the press something—indeed much—of the feeling of an exalted society where choice spirits met face to face, shared the same principles, of truth, honour, integrity, love of country, loyalty, hatred of the base, scorn of the mean: intelligent, beauty-loving, witty, but candid, trustworthy, and arcadian in rural delights. We cannot say but that this was Pope's honest idea of his truest self, and these are the values he promulgates in poem after poem. Moreover, since he is continually addressing a named company in the first person, we, who would uphold the same ideals, have no difficulty in identifying ourselves with that good society, and are uplifted together. While Envy howls, and Flattery sickens, the curtain of black print dissolves, the illusion of union is complete, we are gathered into the artifice of eternity:

Truth guards the poet, sanctifies the line,
And makes immortal, Verse as mean [No, Mr. Pope! as *noble*] as
[thine.][1]

While we read, the spell holds; and, while the spell lasts, we believe.

3

This sympathetic rapport with a known, or at least clearly envisaged, audience was what every man of letters needed to establish, in order to be convincing and successful as a 'creative' writer. But the path to it through printed prose was still uncharted. It is obvious from this distance—but the solution was instinctive—that the way to get in to a public personally unknown was to knock at the front door in person. Written correspondence was normal between friends, useful between strangers, communicable to a third party. All personal letters were in greater or less degree unavoidably autobiographical, and might naturally flow into narrative, with comment on the action at will. Ideally, autobiography was an extended letter to a friend. Point of view was in effect automatic, and one started with an identified audience. These are enormous initial advantages.

The Writer

Letter-writing between friends was clearly congenial to great numbers of English in the eighteenth century—so congenial that probably four-fifths of the best letters in English carry that superscription as to place and time. Circumstances so favourable are by no means to be taken for granted. People lived far enough apart for letters to be wanted and needed, in a dearth of easier, more immediate ways of communication. Town-dwellers do not write to one another, except to invite, accept, and thank. In the country, where obligations (accompaniments of real property) kept you more or less immobile and isolated, letters were a sensible enrichment of the day, able to change its entire complexion, and when you were the recipient you paid as happily for a good long letter as for a ticket to theatre, concert, or ball in town. The pleasure was mutual, and with these incitements letter-writing rose to the level of superb art—a genre of the utmost variety, flexibility, and felicity of expression. The capabilities of English prose have hardly elsewhere, in its whole range, been so inventively and thoroughly, if casually, explored. Cicero and his fellows, in this art if nowhere else, would have to give place. Only to *name* stars of the first magnitude—Chesterfield, Lady Mary, Gray, Walpole, Cowper—is to be convinced of this truth.

In the simplest verbal interchange we have, at the least, the Autocrat's complexity of persons, to be elaborated as we please. For example, there are the 'real' Gray, the 'real' Walpole, Gray's Gray, Walpole's Walpole, Gray's Walpole, and Walpole's Gray. There are also Gray's Walpole's Gray, and Walpole's Gray's Walpole. In this colloquy, the main dialogue proceeds at the second remove, between Gray's Gray and Walpole's Walpole, but prompted by 'moi-mêmes' who have unavowed investments in the venture, and prodded and nudged by the others at unspecified moments, sometimes quite insistently. All these are potentially operative forces on a level of conscious awareness. As for the materials of such interchange, they are as limitless as the purposes prompting their selection: narrative, descriptive, expository, opinionative. Johnson told Mrs Thrale that to write when one had nothing to tell was 'the great epistolick art',[1] and Cowper demonstrated this art in its utmost perfection, not once but often. Every such letter is a dramatic monologue.

We must now try to translate the actual relationships adumbrated in the paradigm suggested, into a not-so-brave *new* world, that of imaginative prose—prose fiction—in the medium of print. It is not surprising that this particular genre should preempt our discussion henceforward. It is at once the most significant product of the changes taking place in that literary world, the most revealing and problematic from a critical point of view, and the most portentous, historically considered. Moreover, especially at the outset, the novel was interrelated with most other reputable forms of literary prose and grew away from them in a haphazard, unpremeditated fashion—not by arbitrary definition or plan. As Saunders says, 'The joy of the novel, *then*, was the same as the joy of the biography, but salted to taste by the ancillary joys associated with essays, real-life letters, true travel stories, histories and other forms. The novel is not a thing apart, but a form of literature which derives inevitably from, and remains integrally interconnected with, the host of the other prose forms in this age of prose'.[2]

We must consider what happens when an unknown X and Y are substituted for the known relations of the paradigmatic original. Let X be the author and Y the reading public, each unknown to the other. Then X's X at once develops a range of possibilities previously denied: (1) X's genuine autobiography; (2) assumption of alien identity, even to shift of sex; (3) fictitious events; (4) opinions on these corresponding to the author's real views; (5) opinions opposite to the author's true ideas and values; (6) a mixture of these options in varying proportions. The reading public must guess the character and intentions of the primary X; and since the public, Y, is a multiple, Y^n, there will be a variety of guesses. But, if the work is a success, Y will guess in the general direction X has predetermined for it. But why? how?

There, of course, lies the heart of the problem: how to establish an understanding, a mutual give-and-take, reciprocity of emotional, intellectual, moral response with a person or persons never seen? The old assurance from proximity has been taken away at a difficult time: just when the literary profession, as profession, is beginning to walk by itself, and when imaginative prose is trying its powers in many new directions. A solid, tangible public would have been fortifying at such a moment. How can an insecure author with a bantling be at home with a Cheshire Cat?

While she was still looking at the place where it had been, it suddenly appeared again. 'By-the-bye, what became of the baby?' said the Cat. 'I'd nearly forgotten to ask.' 'It turned into a pig,' Alice answered very quietly... 'I thought it would,' said the Cat, and vanished again.

[After she had gone some way] Alice looked up, and there was the Cat again, sitting on a branch of a tree. 'Did you say pig, or fig?' said the Cat. 'I said pig,' replied Alice; 'and I wish you wouldn't keep appearing and vanishing so suddenly: you make one quite giddy.' 'All right,' said the Cat; and this time it vanished quite slowly, beginning with the end of the tail, and ending with the grin, which remained some time after the rest of it had gone.[1]

In such circumstances, an act of faith is the first requisite. If the author believes hard enough that the audience is truly there, he may from time to time see it materialise. But he must not look for guidance from it—can only expect hindsight. Knocking at the front door in person is not so easy to do but is part of that act of faith. Since Y doesn't live anywhere in particular, X must trust that he has come to the right lodging, where he or his simulacrum will find a sympathetic welcome. He knocks, and with an asking face presents his credentials in the form of a printed book telling his story. Suppose it begins: 'I was born in the year 1632, in the city of York, of a good family, though not of that country, my father being a foreigner of Bremen, named Kreutznaer, who settled first at Hull.'[2] Y is in his library and does not appear at the door. He glances at the book briefly, sees that it is packed with arresting circumstance which holds one's attention and generates confidence in its veracity. He sends out a few coins to the waiting figure at the door, bids him leave his testimonials and come back another day, after his case has been considered as it may deserve. Whether the author, in whatever guise, will ever find his way back, or learn *Y*'s opinion, is doubtful. Does it matter? Yes!

'But I don't want to go among mad people,' Alice remarked. 'Oh, you can't help that,' said the Cat: 'we're all mad here. I'm mad. You're mad.' 'How do you know I'm mad?' said Alice. 'You must be,' said the Cat, 'or you wouldn't have come here.'[1]

There are two realities, the author and the reader. But they never confront each other in person. The whole transaction takes place in the world of 'Als ob'. It is not a *terra firma*, not at all reassuring to a family man with responsibilities. There must be a way to get closer to the reader. Is it by implying more than appears on the surface of the writing? Is there a promise of a compact, a more intimate relation by signs behind the back, or over the head, of the narrator? Can he be made to speak more than he realises, so that a secret recognition may be exchanged between real author and reader? Watt calls attention[2] to the following passage in *Crusoe*, where the hero is salvaging anything useful he can bring ashore from the wrecked ship:

I smiled to myself at the sight of this money; O drug! I exclaimed, what art thou good for?...e'en remain where thou art, and go to the bottom, as a creature whose life is not worth saving. However, upon second thoughts, I took it away.

Is it an ironic signal from Defoe to the reader? We shall never know. Defoe's inexpressive countenance gives no second sign. Either he does not see the opening or he refuses to follow it up, and our perplexity increases fiftyfold with other impersonations, most notably with Moll Flanders. When this author has fused himself with the imagined person, the process is so remarkably thorough that he seems to have nothing still unexpressed on that subject: to have nothing left over that he wishes to communicate privately. He is content to be measured in the dimensions of his characters, whatsoever obliquities, inconsistencies, or limitations they may display. As an author, he is for the newer generation of running, or bustling, reader—a *public* without privacies—and why should he want a closer relation than what he already enjoyed?

If Defoe is often puzzling because he seems too straightforward to be trusted, Swift is so for the opposite reason. He is for the reader of today, who of course accepts nothing at face value. The world of print was made to order for Swift: it offers him personal anonymity, self-concealment, the means of directing his fire from a selected ambush against any object he may choose. His disguises are innumerable, and in each he discloses only so much of himself as he pleases to reveal. His own point of view is almost never overt, and is usually at the extreme distance from that of his mouthpiece. He is nearly as great a master of matter-of-fact narrative as Defoe, but he uses it for setting springes and gins. Consider the first paragraph of *Lilliput* as a suitable opening for a book of wonders. Thus, in part:

Soon after my return from Leyden [where I studied physic for two years and seven months], I was recommended...to be surgeon to the Swallow, Captain Abraham Pannell, commander, with whom I continued three years and a half...When I came back I resolved to settle in London...I took part of a small house in the Old Jewry; and being advised to alter my condition, I married Mrs Mary Burton, second daughter to Mr Edmund Burton, hosier, in Newgate Street, with whom I received four hundred pounds for a portion.[1]

Swift will always entrap the reader if he can, and delight in the trick. But the reader whom he cannot fool is the one he is really after, *quasi alter ego*. Such a one is his true and private audience. If he can find one such in a thousand readers, he may be pleased; but even so he will not openly acknowledge him, essential to Swift's sufficiency though he be. Irony is the instrument, a sort of Geiger counter, by which he finds out his proper reader. But, though the signals are mutually reciprocated, they generate no warmth. Nor do they always reach conviction. Gulliver's fourth book is a stumbling-block for any who feel themselves sealed of the tribe. How much confidence does he inspire in us that we have read him as he meant?

Of the two authors touched upon, neither, it appears, satisfactorily solved the problem of an author's relations through the opacity of print with an audience of readers. If the authors are content, the reader is not. His side of the connection is left uncertain and incomplete. Defoe's X is crystal-clear and solid but what of Y's, the reader's, Defoe? The last-named takes so little independent room in the picture that, for purposes of the book's contribution to any society, X and Defoe may as well be lumped together. Swift's X, on the contrary, though solid enough to be taken over without change as the reader's X, is so obviously a distortion of the author's meaning that the reader must attempt to resolve the anamorphosis by seeking for Swift himself. But the range of possible inference left open to Y in this element of the equation is too wide to be reduced to comfortable assurance. At the end of the book Swift is still to seek.

It may be possible to establish a closer solidarity between author and reader by means of correspondence, or by adopting the techniques of epistolary interchange. This experiment is tried by Richardson, and then exploited by him with overwhelming success. It drastically modifies, and even transforms, several factors in the configuration. First and foremost, it circumvents the Cheshire Cat. By identifying, characterising, and fixing an audience of named individuals *within* the story itself, Richardson evades, or avoids, the vagueness of address that so constricts and formalises the ordinary autobiographer. He writes to particular people, whose friendly concern may be assumed; who naturally condition what he says and the way he says it. He can count on a response, which itself provides one of the elements of narrative continuity and keeps alive expectation. It relieves the relentless fixation on the first person, develops secondary foci of interest, removes the embarrassment of an appearance of total recall or the subterfuge of an impossibly detailed journal. It provides unforeseen opportunities for reconsideration, in the light of developing events and differing points of view. It makes easy openings for explication and discussion and for the expression of fresh insights.

Moreover, it alters the whole time-scheme with vivid benefits. The temporal range is moved forward into the immediate past, with the excitement of recent events, merging into the passing hour and anxiety for the imminent future. There is little occasion for summoning up a cold past. Emotion, therefore, not recollected in tranquillity, but as reflected in the present pulse-rate, is the element in which the communicated thoughts now live. It animates the writer, the recipient of the letter, and inevitably the new reader at whatever distance. Distance, in fact, of time and place is non-existent while we read, and we move unconsciously into position as the recipient of Clarissa's letters, to which we react with corresponding sentiments.

This is a triumphant annihilation of the barrier between writer and reader. It is, in fact—with the reservation soon to be made—the ideal to which novelists normally aspire—or at least until recently did aspire. To live vicariously another life with such psychological intensity that for a certain time our own is subsumed in the other: this, whatever critical pundits may say, is the goal of a novel-reader in his essentiality. This is the way of children with story-books; this is the experience that the readers of novels in the eighteenth century sought and cherished: this is the characteristic joy of prose-fiction, its promise, its potency, and its danger. At the time when first-rate novels could be counted on the fingers of one hand, what was it that readers of all classes, from the servant-maid to the top levels of sophisticated culture, were seeking from them? Not objects of critical disquisition but vehicles of vicarious experience. We have a perfect opportunity to test the assertion by the voluntary testimony offered to Richardson by Fielding in the letter written after reading the fifth volume of *Clarissa*. After praising the consistency and naturalness of characterisation, Fielding continues:

Shall I tell you? Can I tell you what I think of the latter part of your Volume? Let the Overflowings of a Heart which you have filled brimfull speak for me.

When Clarissa returns to her Lodgings at St Clairs the Alarm begins, and here my Heart begins *its* Narrative. I am Shocked; my Terrors [? rise], and I have the utmost Apprehensions for the poor betrayed Creature.—But when I see her enter with the Letter in her Hand, and after some natural Effects of Despair, clasping her Arms about the Knees of the Villain, call him her Dear Lovelace, desirous and yet unable to implore his Protection or rather his mercy; I then melt into Compassion, and find what is called an Effeminate Relief for my Terror. to continue to the End of the Scene. When I read the next Letter I am Thunderstruck; nor can many Lines explain what I feel from Two.

. . . The Circumstance of the Fragments is Great and Terrible; but her Letter to Lovelace is beyond any thing I have ever read. God forbid that the Man who reads this with dry Eyes should be alone with my Daughter when she hath no Assistance within Call. Here my Terror ends and my Grief begins which the Cause of all my Tumultuous Passions soon changes into Raptures of Admiration and Astonishment by a Behaviour the most Elevated I can possibly conceive, and what is at the same time most Gentle and most natural...During the Continuance of this Vol. my Compassion is often moved; but I think my Admiration more. If I had rec'd no Hint or Information of what is to succeed I should perceive you paving the way to load our admiration of your Heroine to the Highest Pitch, as you have before with wonderfull Art prepared us for both Terror and Compassion on her Account. This last seems to come from the Head. Here then I will end: for I assure you nothing but my Heart can force me to say Half of what I think of the Book.[1]

That, we can hardly doubt, is the way the novel ought to be read, and it is a sincere tribute on a first reading when the work was new.

4

It is to be observed that what has been said of the reader's intimate involvement with Richardson's heroine relates to that precisely. The epistolary form unites us to the characters, not to the author. Clarissa may be a bond of association between us and him, may elevate him in our estimation and arouse our admiration of his genius. Otherwise, it does not bring us to a personal intimacy. That Richardson felt this separation from his audience might be inferred from the great amount of his own writing around and about the novel. He was unwilling to leave it to speak for itself but had to be discussing it with all and sundry, in his own person.

Now, this was an aspect of an author's relation to his public that Fielding was disposed to take upon himself as his immediate concern. He had a great deal to say about his greatest novel, about the forms of fiction, about the conduct of the narrative, about self-appointed critics, about the character and actions of his invented persons, about the conduct of life itself; and he chose to incorporate all this in the body of the novel, in introductory essays, in running comment, and in the witty, wry, ironic manner in which he reported events. He gives us so much of himself that in effect he becomes, not a character in the book, but the Master of Ceremonies, and much the most interesting person in it, if at the same time apart from it. We feel that we know him better, and more intimately, on his own chosen terms, than anyone else to whom we are introduced. Without this personal voice at all times in our ears, the book would be a vastly different sort of thing. This is why he could not have written it, like the other novels so far mentioned, in the first person as a character; and this is why the cinema version, excellent though it be, and faithful up to a point, is so comparatively thin and unsatisfying to the reader of *Tom Jones*, and so entirely different in effect. This is why, though *Robinson Crusoe* might be turned into a movie without much loss—perhaps with perceptible gain—Fielding's novel is in fact untranslatable. The kinship of Fielding and Chaucer has been noted before. It is a truth that Fielding has returned in very characteristic fashion to a close semblance—in spite of prose and print—of the early oral techniques of the great narrative poet. The point need not be laboured. Both authors are conspicuously present on all occasions, as ironic observers and commentators, and as essential parts of the scene and total effect. It is an amusing coincidence, a pretty parallel, that the figure in which Fielding presents himself as author, as he opens his novel, is that of mine host, or 'master of a public ordinary', who offers a bill of fare under the general heading of Human Nature, with chapter titles for particular items, in the antique descriptive manner—as it were a General Prologue with hints of dietary variety in store.

Fielding's solution brings him and the reader into close relationship, and in his hands is so successful as to serve as a model for a great part of the novel-writing of the next century. But it is retrograde from the advance in psychological realism achieved by Richardson's epistolary method. What it gains in propinquity of author and reader, it loses in distance between author and characters. Author and reader remain together outside the story and can only guess at thoughts and motivations by the outward signs. To be sure, Fielding presumes upon his appointed distance not infrequently; but his typical stance will be seen on almost any page. Thus, for example:

It surprises us, and so perhaps it may the reader, that the lieutenant, a worthy and good man, should have applied his chief care rather to secure the offender than to preserve the life of the wounded person. We mention this observation, not with any view of pretending to account for so odd a behaviour...it is our business to relate facts as they are...[1]

The problem, then, is how to fuse the two halves and yet keep them distinct. How can the author identify himself with his characters so closely as to express their thoughts and emotions as they arise, and yet remain free to comment at will on these matters in a comfortable companionship with the reader? How be in the action and out of it at the same time? How be at once first and third person, at once actor and explicator?

This is the paradoxical problem to which Sterne finds a paradoxical solution. 'Writing,' declares Tristram

when properly managed (as you may be sure I think mine is), is but a different name for conversation. As no one, who knows what he is about, in good company would venture to talk all;—so no author, who understands the just boundaries of decorum and good-breeding, would presume to think all. The truest respect which you can pay to the reader's understanding, is to halve this matter amicably, and leave him something to imagine in his turn, as well as yourself.

For my own part, I am eternally paying him compliments of this kind, and do all that lies in my power to keep his imagination as busy as my own.[1]

As a description of Sterne's actual practice in *Tristram Shandy*, this is not at all bad. He goes a stride beyond Richardson along the road of psychological immediacy. Instead of enabling the reader to examine subsequently a series of letters exchanged between persons writing to one another in an imagined present, he adopts the personally immediate address of Fielding to *his* audience, as the author engaged in writing the book. But, since he is writing in the autobiographical mode, he is at the same time the book's nominal hero and the nexus of action. As author, he addresses an immediate audience, and therefore in an immediate present (as one would in a letter). But, as character, he cannot speak to an audience that has no existence within that fictional ambience. He is thus forced to bring his readers inside the book's action and make them part of the proceedings. He can do this only by assuming the contemporaneity of their mutual communications, so that each participant is a part of the other's present. The book therefore reverts in effect to the original condition of oral discourse, and becomes a conversational interchange between speaker and hearer, Sterne's X and Y; which is to say, between Sterne's Tristram and

Sterne's image of ourselves as party to the unfolding of his anecdotes. The style has all the apparent ease and inconsequentiality of the most casual, unpremeditated talk. Since the time of conversation is always current time, is now, the relevant past is drawn into it as an integral component of present consciousness. We are by degrees—in the disconnected fashion in which odd bits of information about our acquaintances are usually acquired—informed of what transpired in Tristram's earlier history and that of his family. But we are not allowed to sit like passive buckets while Tristram fills the void. Sterne's is no idle boast: he *is* 'eternally paying us compliments' of his attention, whether he addresses us as 'Sir', 'Madam', 'My Lord', 'your Reverences', 'my dear friend and companion', or as 'my fellow-labourers and associates in this great harvest of our learning now ripening before our eyes'. He continually includes us in his 'We'; he is always asking us questions and soliciting our views on the point at issue; guessing our thoughts; and even putting the words into our mouths from time to time. For example:

My uncle Toby Shandy, madam, was a gentleman... [of] a most extreme and unparalleled modesty of nature:—though I correct the word nature, for this reason, that I may not prejudge a point which must shortly come to a hearing; and that is, whether this modesty of his was natural or acquired.—Whichever way my uncle Toby came by it, it was nevertheless modesty in the truest sense of it; and that is, madam, not in regard to words... but to things;—and this kind of modesty so possessed him... as almost to equal, if such a thing could be, even the modesty of a woman,—that female nicety, madam, and inward cleanliness of mind and fancy, in your sex, which makes you so much the awe of ours.

You will imagine, madam, that my uncle Toby had contracted all this from this very source;—that he had spent a great part of his time in converse with your sex; and that, from a thorough knowledge of you, and the force of imitation which such fair examples render irresistible,—he had acquired this amiable turn of mind.

I wish I could say so... no, he got it, madam, by a blow.—A blow!—

Yes, madam, it was owing to a blow from a stone, broke off by a ball from the parapet of a horn-work at the siege of Namur, which struck full upon my uncle Toby's groin.—Which way could that affect it?—The story of that, madam, is long and interesting;—but it would be running my history all upon heaps to give it you here.—[1]

Beyond this degree of involvement of the reader in the conduct of the narrative it seems hardly possible to go. If the primary object be to bring the author and unknown reader into the closest working relation, this seems to be the *ne plus ultra*.

But the sacrifices resulting from Sterne's method are equally conspicuous. At a stroke, it reduces the plot, or story content, to a level of second-rate interest. Progressive though the digressions may be, narrative suspense and expectation are done away with, except for brief episodes: no one ever read *Tristram Shandy* through to find how it comes out. And, if the sequence of events is given over for a continuous present, the development of character is also surrendered. The interest in the character of the 'hero' is all of a piece throughout, and really slight; while the most memorable parts of the book are third-personal episodes that do not much benefit from the novelties of Sterne's method but conform to the old-fashioned continuities of character description, action, scene and dialogue.

After Sterne's *succès fou* with the first two volumes, he did of course become personally acquainted with the cream of his reading public and doubtless joined in abundance of good talk. But all this social experience had little perceptible effect on the artistic method, which proceeded up hill and down dale as inspiration drove or flagged. Since time present galloped faster than time past, he was, as he humorously pointed out, losing ground all the while in the recounting his own life-story, and might go on with it as long as breath continued. But the fictitious collocation of author and audience remained as before.

5

The novel-writers of the eighteenth century did not, to my knowledge, discover any other kinds of author/reader relationship than those exemplified by the five great masters so far considered. The autobiographical novel in the first person continued to find favour, since it offered infinite variety in the choice of protagonist, with consequent identification of the reader and hero, to whatsoever degree. *The Vicar of Wakefield*, autobiographical in form, is original in displaying a refined and sympathetic irony from its memorable opening to the concluding paragraph. The amiable complacency of the Vicar, who must be supposed to possess full knowledge of all the subsequent events of the tale before he begins telling—a tale that offers little justification for his optimistic views of life—is conveyed with a delicacy inimitable and sweet. We love the author who can approach us in a semblance so irresistibly appealing: we feel close to him by virtue of the affectionate gratitude he inspires.

It will hardly be argued that the exploitation of eccentric protagonists, human (as John Buncle), animal or inanimate (as Pompey the Little or Chrysal), taught much about either life or novelistic techniques. The novelty of the angle of vision offers no unusual illumination, nor any unfamiliar relation of author and audience.

The novel *à clé*, or scandalous romance, dependent on private information shared by author and reader, is analogous to the satiric tradition in that it is to be, as it were, translated. While it puts writer and reader in a closet together with the door closed, this intimacy is not truly productive of a mutual sympathy. Once the reader is possessed of the key, he takes little interest in matters (if any exist) aside from the main affair—or in the author himself—and discards the book like a sucked orange.

The moral fable and the Eastern Tale, both much practised and favoured in our period, can be illustrated with masterpieces, notably Johnson's; but they have designs on the reader of a kind different from those with which we are here mainly concerned, and must be put by. The author/reader relationship generated by the apologue is analogous to pulpit and congregation, a benevolent condescension and a willing submission. They are extended *exempla* in an undelivered sermon.

The further exploitation of the epistolary method produced occasional triumphs, like *Humphry Clinker* and *Evelina*, but I think no new insights. The novels that followed the central road of third-personal narrative, like *The Spiritual Quixote*, did not rise to the level of their great 'prose-epical' prototype, entertaining though they often are. Of most examples of the picaresque style much the same can be said. The pursuit of Sterne's eccentric path proved a blind alley to his immediate imitators and successors. We remember Johnson's pronouncement: 'Nothing odd will do long. Tristram Shandy did not last.'[1] This was doubtless true— and undisputed by Boswell—at the time it was spoken. But the oddity of the book was the least permanent thing about it.

6

A generation of novel-readers trained on the prefaces of Henry James does not need to be reminded that the paramount technical problem which has exercised the ingenuity of novelists for the last century has been how to obliterate the reader's consciousness of the author during the reading of his book, so that the work can pass directly into vicarious experience without any apparent intermediary. This was very far from being Sterne's object. Although he couched his fiction in first-personal terms, he meant the subterfuge to be transparent. The events of Tristram's personal history may be fanciful, but the whimsical cast of his mind is virtually indistinguishable from that of his author, and what he has to say about life and the techniques of composition is identical with what Sterne himself professed. In this respect, therefore, he was moving rather up- than down-stream, as the subsequent history of the novel—unless for three-quarters of a century we have been in a confounding backwater—seems to show. What Sterne did positively and memorably demonstrate, however, was the unsuspectedly small part rational order played in human affairs: how inevitably imperfect and fallible were the efforts of verbal communication and how comically mistaken was the assumption of mutual understanding in any the most common interchange of ideas. The exploration of unreason was a disturbingly fruitful line of development for the future of the novel. Once this conception had thoroughly permeated the vulgar consciousness, all that was called for was the indefatigable erection of monuments to our insignificance.

Sterne's other major innovation, the overt injection of the reader into the texture of his design, was, like his self-portraiture, against the current. As the novel has grown to maturity, it has gained in self-assurance as the dominant art-form. With the growth of the fiction-reading public to unimagined size, it has become evident that the competent practitioner need never worry about finding readers. Consequently, he has ceased to be preoccupied with the problem of public relations, and has retreated further and further into the cave of his privacy, whence from time to time issue sibylline utterances which the eager seeker after esoteric experience may interpret as he likes. Far from admitting his responsibility to convey any personal convictions, the modern novelist flatters himself with their concealment, and denies to the reader the right to impute to *him* any moral or other statement that his characters may express or imply. The veil of print has finally thickened to inviolability, and the separation of author and reader is as total as the former can contrive to make it.

Oddly enough, the reader, formerly the object of the author's solicitude, does not resent this reversal of responsibility but reveres it. So the present-day reader pursues the novelist into his secret lair in search of wisdom, confident that inaccessibility is the seal of wisdom. In this he resembles my Father Shandy:

As the dialogue was of Erasmus, my father...read it over and over again, with great application, studying every word and every syllable of it through and through in its most strict and literal interpretation.— He could still make nothing of it, that way. Mayhap there is more meant than is said in it, quoth my father.—Learned men, brother Toby, don't write dialogues upon long noses for nothing.—I'll study the mystic and the allegoric sense.—Here is some room to turn a man's self in, brother.[1]

The reader is not easily balked, these days. Saul Bellow recently expressed his impatience with the tendency of contemporary society to deify, or at least to hallow, the artist. 'We look to the artist', he is reported as saying to a campus audience, 'to transmit new modes of conduct, to supply ideas, clues, hints; to provide a form of life. We have made artists a privileged class, a breed of holy men who have replaced the lives of the saints. Artists are more envied than millionaires, they are beyond authority, for them the rules are waived.'[2] It is to be noted parenthetically that this deification usually results from word-of-mouth fame, not word-of-critics: a sub-variety of oral tradition.

Thus the whirligig of time brings in his revenges. From having been a pursuer after a valid relation with his audience, the author has become the pursued, and for the same reason. The ancient need of a personal bond between author and audience still exerts its force. The satisfactions of a relation through the medium of print are not sufficient. We still want the closer connection: the face, the living voice, the charisma of a physical presence that we can touch. Why does a successful author attract the crowds when he goes on the University Circuit as lecturer? Why does every announcement of a new novel in the Sunday supplement have to be accompanied with a photograph of the author thereof? What is the audience-motivation in the publishers' Meet-the-Author parties? Why are TV interviews with authors so much in demand?—'I found his book interesting. What is he really like?' The book will not tell. But also, disregarding financial profit, is there not still a felt need on the author's part to come face to face with his embodied audience, to gauge their attitudes and qualities, like a dramatist's wish to see and hear the response to his play? McLuhan quotes John O'Hara's words in *The New York Times Book Review*, 27 November 1955:

You know your reader is captive inside those covers, but as novelist you have to imagine the satisfaction he's getting. Now, in the theater —well, I used to drop in during both productions of *Pal Joey* and watch, not imagine, the people enjoy it.[1]

It appears, then, that the problems latent in the medium of the printed word have not yet been worked out to the mutual satisfaction of author and audience. The difficulties with which the eighteenth-century novelists wrestled are still with us. The deprivation they encountered was serious. It was a loss of a vital, meaningful, and responsible connection mutually acknowledged. With the changed conditions of the world of print, time-honoured and traditional values had been alienated almost without anyone's fully realising what was taking place. The gulf-stream, as it were, had shifted outward and the climate would be different thereafter.

The vital and meaningful aspects of the old relation are visible in every worthwhile personal association. What they contributed to literature is evident in the best of our earlier poetry and drama, and very visible in the private letters of the century upon which we have come to confer. The responsibility to which we allude is primarily moral. The menace to it implicit in the separation was never better expressed than by Johnson, in his fourth *Rambler* essay, which excites the indignant protest of today's graduate students, who invariably misread it. 'If the world', he declares,

be promiscuously described, I cannot see of what use it can be to read the account; or why it may not be as safe to turn the eye immediately upon mankind, as upon a mirror which shows all that presents itself without discrimination...Many writers, for the sake of following nature, so mingle good and bad qualities in their principal personages, that they are both equally conspicuous; and as we accompany them through their adventures with delight, and are led by degrees to interest ourselves in their favour, we lose the abhorrence of their faults... To this fatal error all those will contribute, who confound the colours of right and wrong... In narratives where *historical* veracity has no place, I cannot discover why there should not be exhibited the most perfect *idea* of virtue; of virtue not angelical, nor above probability, for what we cannot credit we shall never imitate, but the highest and purest that humanity can reach, which... may, by conquering some calamities, and enduring others, teach us what we may hope, and what we can perform. Vice, for vice is necessary to be shewn, should always disgust... Wherever it appears, it should raise hatred. [He has already suggested a reason that was more adequate, though not more apt, in his own time than today: 'These books are written chiefly to the young, the ignorant, and the idle, to whom they serve as lectures of conduct, and introductions into life. They are the entertainment of minds un-furnished with ideas... not fixed by principles... not informed by experiences...' He concludes:] There are thousands of readers of romances willing to be thought wicked, if they may be allowed to be wits. It is therefore to be steadily inculcated, that virtue is the highest *proof* of understanding, and the only *solid* basis of greatness; and that vice is the natural consequence of *narrow* thoughts, that it begins in mistake, and ends in ignominy.

If we have travelled far, it is along the road that Johnson fore-saw. What he reprobates, Stendhal adopts as a definition of the genre.[1] As Wayne Booth, condemning Céline's best-known work in his admirable *Rhetoric of Fiction*, comments:

inside views can build sympathy even for the most vicious character... it is hardly surprising that works in which this effect [impersonal narration] is used have often led to moral confusion... too often for us to dismiss moral questions as irrelevant to technique... Caught in the trap of a suffering consciousness, we are led to succumb morally as well as visually... we cannot excuse [Céline] for writing a book which, if taken seriously by the reader, must corrupt him... Taken seriously, the book would make life itself meaningless except as a series of self-centred forays into the lives of others.[2]

The contemporary abrogation of moral responsibility on the part of the author, in favour of novel excitations of 'reader participation', is one of the results of the separation and consequent mutual privacy of the acts of writing for print alone and of solitary reading. It is difficult to believe that an art which by this kind of enablement has so far outpaced the currently accepted mores of a permissive society can go much further in the same direction. We may rather hope and expect, in the light of such abundant evidence of unquenchable need to break through the barriers of print, that there will come a fresh effort toward the re-establishment—inside the literary forms themselves, and not for mere cabinet exhibition—of a mutually candid, cordial, and honourably responsible relationship between the author and his chosen audience.

CHAPTER 7

COMMENTARY

Summarised by James L. Clifford

The answers to the nagging questions posed in the preface must now seem fairly obvious. The experts did react to the challenge with astonishing uniformity. Only in the last paper, concerned with the 'writer', was there any major divergence of approach. Here Bertrand Bronson chose to interpret the problem in purely literary terms. Yet even his essay is not fundamentally at odds with the general conclusion.

How can we phrase it? Instead of the traditional 'Yes—but' explanation, stressing the major accomplishments of the century with a few reservations, the speakers chose to concentrate on the unhappy plight of the individual in eighteenth-century society. This was 'No—but'. In most areas there were crippling restrictions on individual expression, but there were a few encouraging signs. Little doubt was left of the experts' overall opinion of the traditional labels, or what they thought of the implications of such terms as Saintsbury's 'The Peace of the Augustans', an oversimplification which must be eradicated.

In contradiction to the old erroneous vision of the eighteenth century as a complacent island of elegant assurance, with comfortable existence for all levels of society, life for the ordinary man must have been one of uncertainty and insecurity. For all our later emphasis on the miserable living and working conditions brought on by the industrial revolution, these nevertheless represented, as Dorothy George pointed out long ago and T. S. Ashton more recently, an improvement over the way the masses had previously lived. Too often we have been misled by literary fictions and political oversimplifications.

Of course, there were ameliorating factors. Although unlikely to have been able to vote in elections, in a time when the franchise was unusually restricted, the ordinary artisan was becoming more politically conscious. Through effective mob violence and through the printed word, he was gradually learning to exert mass power, which eventually led to nineteenth-century reform. In what was for the few a gentleman's utopia, the lot of the poor man was grim, *but* it was at least better than that of his counterpart on the Continent. The eighteenth-century church, as G. R. Cragg admitted, was not so bad all of the time as it was some of the time. British artists, whose social prestige had been deplorable, were beginning to organise, and their conditions were improving. If musical composition was at a low ebb, London, none the less, was one of the musical capitals of the world, a mecca for continental artists. Only in literature is this overall summation somewhat blurred. The material position of the average author was certainly improving, though still, by twentieth-century standards, leaving much to be desired. But the new commercial society and the wider audience produced by cheap printing had destroyed the close relationship of author and reader. New techniques of writing were demanded, and the eighteenth century turned into an experimental era where diverse fictional approaches were being tried out. The old renaissance humanistic intimacy was disappearing, *but* new relationships were being discovered.

To be sure, for many readers this 'No—but' interpretation may seem too arbitrary and facile. Even so basic an antithesis falsifies the record. It would be safer not to attempt any overall summation, although one could easily point out such general areas of agreement as the increased social conscience, the deepening affluence of the urban middle classes, the question of growing radicalism. One could show how Hogarth's prints, subscription concerts, art exhibitions, the increasing popularity of the novel and the beginnings of a really extensive interest in economic and political concerns and in newspapers and pamphlets are all reflections of this social change. But this is to belabour the obvious. More useful here may be to discuss the reactions of other scholars who attended the conference.

For various reasons it has seemed expedient not to include all of the discussion which followed each paper. Admirable though much of it was, a large amount had to do with very special problems or focused on matters only incidentally bearing on the subject. Yet it would appear of some value, especially for students, to provide a running commentary which embodies the more significant points made by those who spoke. Readers will thus be able at least to get some sense of the direction of the argument.

I

Harvey C. Mansfield, Jr, admittedly speaking as a political scientist, began by raising the question of the possibility of isolating one country and period. What is Britain? According to the practicing historian,

Britain can be understood only as it moves. The forms of understanding, the periods, must be gathered like the concept of modern physics, from the moving thing. The thing itself (the essential 'Britain') is of little importance; it may even disappear. For the historian, it is true rather that Britain *is* its history, than that Britain is some unchanging thing which has a history. The period is the concept, the projection, the painting (in the modern sense of the artist's production) of the historian which formulates the movement of Britain...

But we should then be confronted with a series of self-sufficient periods divided by unexplained leaps, the atmosphere of each period consisting of breath many times respired and poisonous to the inhabitants of any other period. The historian, however, is intolerant of leaps. Leaps would destroy continuity, and continuity is the necessary companion of formless change. If 'Britain' were able to leap, she would land beyond the horizon of the historian, who, having no formed picture of Britain, cannot afford to let her out of his sight for an instant. That is why the student of the untold detail and the forgotten worthy makes not merely a contribution to history, but obeys the supreme law of its discipline: omit nothing. 'Britain' needs the concepts of periods to be intelligible, but it also needs the continuity of periods to remain recognisable.

A useful clue, Mansfield then suggested, to the proper study of any period lies in the Aristotelian notion that every society or culture takes its stamp or its mould from its politics. Human change may thus be made more intelligible through a study of changes in regimes. Historical periods would then be thought of as a sequence of regimes, and not merely as reigns, as with chroniclers.

By identifying who rules as the central fact of a society, the political scientist allows for the cultural sameness of 'Britain' while accounting for the greater importance of change. For him the essential Britain is the political Britain which changes; and he does not have to fear that, if the essential Britain changes, 'Britain' is out of sight. He is not afflicted with the gradualism of the historian which explains away change, because having found the central fact in society—its political form—he can demote to accident whatever does not affect this central fact. He can also distinguish planned from unplanned change because he is free of the necessity to explain a new period by a transition in an old period.

This led Mansfield to comment more specifically on J. H. Plumb's paper on Political Man. He took the example of the Revolution of 1688, which seems to have made a noticeable change unobtrusively, 'as if it had been made to ensure the employment of the same or a similar cast in a new play', to support his claim for relating periods to changes in political regime.

The old question whether the Revolution of 1688 was really a revolution must be reopened if the eighteenth century is to be understood as a period. The dominant view today (which Professor Plumb's paper could not but embody) is that eighteenth-century Britain was an unconscious creation of the seventeenth century, until it began unconsciously to create the nineteenth. My understanding leads me to reconsider the Whig view, without the Whiggish hesitations, that the Revolution of 1688 began a new period by founding a new form of government.

This was limited government, not in its modern elaboration as expounded by the American Civil Liberties Union, but as opposed to the only practical alternative of that time, divine right. Divine right, broadly considered, is the view that government has the power and duty to enforce the commands of God. This was the view of both sides of the English Civil War, Puritan and Cavalier, and indeed it was until quite modern times the dominant view in nearly all societies. The rejection of this view makes eighteenth-century Britain a new period of an importance and novelty partly appreciated by the Whig historians and best understood by Montesquieu. Montesquieu called eighteenth-century Britain 'the regime of liberty', and showed how its encouragement of commerce and its policy of secular and latitudinarian toleration created the liberal society required by its limited government.

Plumb had stressed the growth of radical movements in the later eighteenth century as the real revolution. Mansfield, on the other hand, argued that

in the seventeenth century, what we today call 'the social issue' was the issue of church organisation and reform. There were Puritan democrats in that century who wished to democratise 'society', but they intended a change from one form of divine right to another. Their democracy was almost as far from liberal or representative democracy as was the Stuart divine right. The significance of 1688, then, was not the change from absolute monarchy to narrow oligarchy (which might be small) but from divine right to limited government. Before society could be democratised, as we know democracy, it had to be liberalised. Before the social issue could arise as historians know it, the religious issue had to be settled politically.

Mansfield concluded that we should look at the problem from the perspective of the seventeenth, rather than the twentieth century. This is the perspective of men living at the time of change, and it can be captured best by concentrating on the basic issue of divine right.

Plumb was asked to elaborate further on the process by which the party system, which had seemed to be developing in the early eighteenth century, died out by mid-century. To this the speaker answered that in a sense the party system remained, but the trouble was the cost of elections, often involving prodigious sums. Even the well-to-do gentleman could not afford frequent elections. Thus it was easier to have a series of compromises. Instead of dissolutions of parliament there were negotiations and arrangements.

Another query had to do with the survival of small discussion groups which were politically minded, such as debating clubs and cliques that met more or less frequently at coffee houses and taverns. Here Plumb suggested that the question required closer study. There were, of course, Whig- or Tory-dominated meeting places, and, in the latter part of the period, bands of radical reformers. Even musical clubs were used to bring people together who were politically in agreement. Some research is now being done on this topic, and much more should be undertaken.

2

The discussion following Jacob Viner's paper on the economic aspect revealed little difference of opinion. Albert H. Imlah, the initial commentator, considered it a masterly analysis. His only doubt, on a first reading, was whether the shading was a bit too dark, the overall effect tending, for example, to leave the spurt of industrial innovation towards the end of the century—what W. W. Rostow calls the 'take-off' into sustained growth[1]—as something of a miracle rather than an historical development. A second reading had dissipated this small doubt. Viner stressed the period before 1776. In this framework it is quite correct, for example, to emphasise the almost complete absence of government support for education in England and to indicate the narrow limits of aid to the charity schools for the poor. This does not imply that there were no other educational facilities in England itself, or in Scotland.

Commentary

Imlah then pointed out that Viner's preference for honest and intelligent contemporary conjecture had been validated by some recent statistical investigations—those of John T. Krause on demographic change.[1]

His evidence, drawn mainly from parish records in various parts of England, strongly supports the views of eighteenth-century observers such as Adam Smith and Arthur Young, contrary to those of many modern economic historians, that population growth in England in the eighteenth century was more a matter of a rise in fertility than of a decline in the death rate and was in large part the fruit of early marriage under the stimulus of economic changes. For instance, Lancashire, with its growth in textiles and in population, shows relatively early marriage and high birth rates, as do also, it may be noted, the areas of large enclosures and of high poor rates. There seems to have been relatively little immigration into Lancashire, at least from the south. One need not assume, as it has long been fashionable to do, that the enclosure movement forced agricultural labour to the cities. In fact, a large agricultural force was needed in reorganizing and expanding farmlands. Of course, with respect to contemporary observers, one must be discriminating—Adam Smith and Arthur Young, not Goldsmith of 'The Deserted Village'.

Another point which was alluded to by Imlah, and later amplified by various participants, was the matter of education for the poor. Although admittedly coming largely after the period Viner had been discussing, there were signs of increased professional training. And it was the impression of many that the nature of this movement was of some importance to the present discussion. For example, it was pointed out that many manufacturers employing the poor were becoming concerned with the training and motivation of their labourers. Josiah Wedgwood and the Strutts, and others like them, found that the poor would work better if they had not only better discipline but also rewards for superior productivity. From the start Wedgwood was involved in devising bonuses in order to spur his workers to greater efforts. Furthermore, they had to be educated, and he brought in teachers. The Strutts were actively teaching their boys to read and write in the Sunday schools. Thus the entrepreneurs of the later eighteenth century, a few of them at any rate, were getting involved in a new sort of relationship with their poor, which depended on the common man's being more educated and better paid so that he could produce even greater profits for those who employed him.

Viner later examined this question in some detail. Although admitting that it is difficult to be certain about such matters, he added:

I am not sure that there was net improvement in education in the eighteenth century. I know persons who seem to be authorities that tell me that literacy was less prevalent in 1840 than in 1640, and I know that as late as 1840 40 per cent of the working classes in Manchester signed their marriage certificates with a cross. I do not think that would have been true in 1640. The Puritan aspect would have forced parents in some way or other to find a way of reading the *Bible* and teaching children how to read it.

Moreover, he insisted that he had said nothing which precluded the existence of dissenters' academies, or qualified their excellence, as compared, say, with Oxford and Cambridge. But, he continued,

I spoke about the absence of government support of education, and I know of no appropriation of money by the English government, the government of London, for education of any kind, whether for the poor, rich, or middle class, until in the 1840s.

Basic, of course, to a proper understanding of the economic aspect of life in eighteenth-century Britain is a continuing emphasis on property and property rights. It was implied by both Plumb and Viner; and Imlah mentioned, as casual examples, that Dr Johnson grudgingly justified a double standard in sex partly on the basis of property rights, and that John Wilkes rallied military force during the Gordon riots to defend property, including that of the judge (Lord Mansfield) who a few years before had sentenced Wilkes to fine and imprisonment.[1]

3

In the discussion which followed the paper on the position of the Church in the eighteenth century Lewis A. Dralle came to the defence of Bishop Hoadly, who, he thought, had been presented by Cragg in too scandalous colours. As Dralle pointed out, the bishop suffered from a very bad physical malformation, which made it impossible for him to preach except when on his knees. He has been too harshly judged by those who concentrate on his deficiencies as a bishop, and forget his medical history. Cragg insisted that Hoadly was the supreme example of the worldly-mindedness he had claimed in his paper. The fact of Hoadly's physical infirmity was quite true. This made it impossible for him to visit any of his dioceses. But, knowing this, he should never have accepted the bishopric, since he could not act his pastoral part. Yet it would have been inconceivable that any ambitious man in the eighteenth century who was offered a bishopric would decline it. Thus from one point of view he cannot be blamed. But Cragg continued:

The people to be blamed are those who offered him a bishopric. But the reason they offered him a bishopric was because he was the foremost political pamphleteer of the time. I think this is the revealing thing about Hoadly; it illuminates the assumptions which form the mental background of his career. He certainly achieved one thing. He arrested the attention of his constituency. The Bangorian Controversy elicited an amazing number of contributions. The big three-volume folio edition of Hoadly's works devotes nearly twenty double-columned pages to a list of the titles of the books and pamphlets written to refute him. Very few works evoke that kind of response.

In conclusion, Cragg came back to the whole problem of the complacent clergyman, and referred to the account of Simon Patrick, when promoted to the see of Chichester, hugging himself for his good fortune and thanking God for it. Yet this is not by any means the whole story. On the other side is a man like William Law.

People like Simon Patrick never wholly forgot Law, and certainly Law never forgot people like Hoadly. I think the problem was basically one of institutional involvement in society; the people who served the institution participated in its life in a variety of ways and often found it very difficult successfully to disentangle the different strands of activity and emphasis.

4

In beginning the discussion of Rudolf Wittkower's paper on the Artist, Ronald H. Paulson suggested that two related subjects should be considered: the artist as an individual versus society, and man versus society as depicted in the artist's own work. Moreover, he pointed out, a distinction might be made between a man's prestige and his financial prosperity. While admitting that he could think of no prestigious artist who was not also well off, Paulson added that he could think of several who became wealthy without achieving much real prestige. And finally he suggested that there is the central problem of what the artist thought of himself.

Certainly everyone will admit, as the main speaker had clearly shown, that in this period the place of the artist was cruelly ambiguous. Despite the fact that works of art were universally admired, and thus the reputation of artists in general was high, the opportunities for an English practitioner were limited. Cut off from traditional renaissance opportunities, as court painters or designers of altar pieces, he had to seek new ways of achieving success and yet at the same time retain some position in society. Still the most admired genre was history painting, yet for this the English painter was neither apt, nor assured of a steady market. What could he do? One solution was that adopted by Sir Joshua Reynolds. As Paulson commented, what he did was to 'move his peripheral subject to the centre of the stage and pass off the burgher as a king, hero, or saint. Reynolds made the portrait an equivalent of history painting by turning the nondescript middle-class Englishman into a heroic shape in the Grand Style'.[1]

Commentary

The opposite solution was Hogarth's—to point out the inappropriateness of history painting to contemporary English life, by stressing realistic social values instead. Although this brought him fame and fortune, it did not carry with it recognition as a great artist. As Paulson put it,

Here we have the paradox of Hogarth's career. The only role he could see for the artist which would keep him in the centre of his society—not peripheral, as he believed the phiz-mongers (as he called them) to be—was that of a moral censor. And, in this sense, he remained central to his society in a way no other painter of his time could, but he was regarded by the connoisseurs of painting as only peripheral, the ingenious employer of a secondary genre of minor importance.

What must be stressed is the existence in eighteenth-century society of two distinct groups: the great uninformed mass, and a small coterie of learned connoisseurs and critics. Hogarth appealed more to the former, and thus, Paulson continued, 'It is possible for Hogarth to embody both the middle-class success story *and* the prototype of the Romantic artist, neglected and misunderstood. He is the independent artist standing not against society in general but against a coterie.' Most of the people who bought his prints were on his side. Here, then, is a man versus one part of society, suffering injured feelings if not a restricted pocket book.

On the other point—the struggle of the individual in society as depicted in the artist's own works—Paulson suggested that Reynolds again was a useful example. Basically what Sir Joshua accomplished was a subtle heroicising of the English middle class. It is thus possible to consider him as much of a propagandist as Hogarth, but in a different way. The greater part of his work glorified the English ruling class, and incidentally the painter himself, who was so admirably 'applying the forms of Titian and Raphael, the literary allusions, and the elegance of shared social forms to his subjects'.

Naturally, placing ordinary Englishmen in heroic poses called for tremendous tact. No friction between man and society must appear. Man must appear to dominate society. Doing so strengthens his complacence and self-esteem. It panders to his 'sanguine self-image'. Is it possible, one may wonder, that this harmonising of man and society in the portraits of Reynolds and Gainsborough is one of the sources for the later oversimplified generalisations about which we have been complaining? 'The Peace of the Augustans' faces us over and over again in the noble beings in these portraits, surrounded by their faithful animals, placed against the background of flawless nature.

In contrast, Hogarth shows man violently at odds with his surroundings. 'Musicians are confronted by a society of noise-makers, and a poet is pursued even to his attic by duns and hungry dogs.' This is man trying to rise above his present social position, and being 'overcome by recalcitrant Nature'.

In the discussion which followed there was some elaboration of the importance of Hogarth in the struggle to secure copyright protection for etchers and print makers. This was the artisan's way of emancipating himself from aristocratic patronage and putting himself in the hands of the public. Legal protection was necessary as a defence against widespread pirating of popular prints, endangering his source of steady income. Involved, too, was the status of the engraver. Was print-making ever worthy the appellation of high art? For the most part, during the eighteenth century engravers were not taken seriously, even by their fellow artists, and were excluded from membership in the Royal Academy. Only a limited number could become associates. It was not until the nineteenth century that the situation changed. Thus Hogarth, in his copyright struggles, was fighting not only for his own financial security, but also for the elevation of his chief medium of expression, for recognition of superior engravings as high art.

Wittkower was asked to elaborate on the functioning of a portrait-painter's atelier. He explained that we do know quite a lot about the workings of some of the eighteenth-century workshops.

Commentary

The execution of paintings was determined by the price the patron was prepared to pay and the reputation of the painter. In Reynolds's case, for instance, we know exactly how the price chart moved up. At the beginning of his career he charged 5 guineas a head; somewhat later, 12 guineas a head, 24 guineas for a half length and 48 for a whole length; at the end of his career he increased his prices to 50, 100 and 200 guineas respectively. Often dress, hands and background were painted by assistants, who could do nothing else, and Reynolds and others were not very generous to these people. At the beginning of the century portraits were handled in precisely the same way. For instance, in Kneller's portraits very often there is little by Kneller, except perhaps the face. Maybe 70 per cent of Kneller's work was painted by these underlings, who never advanced, whose names are hardly known, or quite unknown, who were badly paid, and never escaped from this drudgery.

Actually, as Wittkower admitted, this tradition goes back to the late Middle Ages and continued through the Renaissance. There was nothing specifically English about the practice. Another participant asked if there were others in the atelier doing even more menial tasks such as drying paint and mixing. The answer was that for centuries the practice was for aspiring artists to enter the workshop at the age of twelve or thirteen, and spend the first two or three years doing nothing but preparing canvases, mixing colours, and so on. Conditions for the most part had not changed.

5

Donald Grout began the discussion of Paul Henry Lang's paper on the place of the composer by quoting from a remark once made by one of his teachers. The English, he said, have always suffered from an unrequited love of music. But why? Lang insisted that one of the chief reasons that English composers in the eighteenth century produced so little great music was that grand opera was in bad repute. England had no indigenous serious opera, which in other countries provided the stimulus for much musical composition. On this point Grout ventured a mild protest, pointing out that circumstances in France at the same time were equally hostile to opera, at least as far as the spirit was concerned.

The strictures against opera by Addison and Steele, Dr Johnson and others in England were matched, if not over-matched, by equally pungent fighting remarks by Saint-Évremond and other French literary figures of the time. Is the reason that France did have opera in spite of this natural antipathy to some drama simply that in France there was a centralised monarchy, a tradition of academies, and the possibility of establishing an opera for the sake of glorifying the ruler?

Or was it the serious satirical spirit which existed in England that was antithetical to romantic musical productions? Or, Grout continued, was it possibly sheer, genetic chance?

Were there no geniuses in England in the eighteenth century who might have done what Purcell did in the seventeenth century under equally discouraging conditions? Were there geniuses in England who simply failed for lack of opportunity to be heard? Or was the situation one of those in which the original inventive minds of the time were attracted into fields which enjoyed a higher social prestige than the fields of musical composition?...There were also fields of development in ensemble instrumental music, in keyboard music—there was the great tradition of organ in Germany which Bach carried on. These two, particularly the tradition of keyboard music, had been great in England in the Elizabethan period and in the early seventeenth century. Why did not this revive after the Restoration? And why did not this take its place in English musical life of the eighteenth century?

Grout could not refrain from asking another question, although admitting that it was unanswerable. What might have happened if Handel in the late 1720s and 1730s had suddenly decided to change from the kind of Italian operas in the baroque style he had learned to compose as a youth, to the new type of Italian operas then being developed on the Continent? Might he possibly have been the leader in England of a radically new native school of dramatic composition? No one can tell. The facts are that he did not, and went on to oratorio instead.

Commentary

Basically, Grout agreed with Lang that, although infertile in composition, England did make certain contributions. In the first place, it played the role of patron and consumer of music, if not of producer. The English paid the bills. The situation might very well be compared to that of the United States in the first few decades of the twentieth century, where foreign artists were welcomed, but where there was no major production of serious music.

Yet it could be claimed that in certain genres eighteenth-century England and early twentieth-century U.S.A. did make genuine contributions. Grout suggested that England in the eighteenth century produced the ballad opera and the glee. The musical comedy in our day has been 'one of the most fruitful, interesting, and original channels of musical composition'. The glee, which in its later stages corresponds more or less with the kind of music popular in Rotary Clubs and perpetuated by the Society for the Preservation of Barber Shop Singing, is characteristic of the type of civilisation in which emphasis is largely upon commercialism. But compositions of this sort are never taken very seriously by musicologists. Thus there is a certain paradox. Grout acknowledged that English music in the eighteenth century was 'poverty-stricken' in one sense; but it made important contributions to the larger realm of musical composition. The picture painted by Lang, Grout continued, shows that this paradox is due to the traditional manner of writing musical history. We tend to concentrate on beatified masterpieces, while the everyday practice of music, and the many minor masters who actually carry the burden of this practice, are slighted. If the music of eighteenth-century England were examined—and made known—to its full extent, Grout suggested, we might have a more realistic view of the situation.

In reply Lang agreed to almost all that Grout had said, but added that, because of the exceptional position of opera in eighteenth-century music, all values are relative. The English would not accept opera, especially Italian opera, and, since all genres of contemporary music were influenced by this form and since operatic *musical idiom* ruled all music, they severely limited their field of action. This opposition to opera was due to literary and moral views. A country with a highly developed theatrical culture will not take kindly to a form of the theatre that is 'all sung'. As a matter of fact, the French were opposed to opera on the same grounds. Addison and the other early critics of opera derived most of their arguments from the French, chief among them Saint-Évremond, perhaps the first critical essayist, who lived in London. The eventual success of the lyric stage in France was attributable to court influence and to the musical and political skill of Lully.

There was in England an additional important limitation which did not exist for the Italians. The Italian wants a show, whether in the church or in the theatre, and usually the same musicians functioned in both. England with its Protestant tradition insisted on gravity and decorum, which excluded any such combination, and undoubtedly this inhibited the natural development of English music.

Someone from the floor asked if the decline in English music might be connected with the dearth of education in the arts in the universities. Only partly, replied Lang. There was always musical training in the English universities, but after Elizabethan times it gradually centred around church music. Oxford and Cambridge produced organists and choirmasters who *also* composed, and by the eighteenth century there was scarcely any attempt made to create contemporary music, or music that looked ahead. Lang further elaborated on the difference between musical education then and now.

To another question, whether Handel (accused of stifling English music) was not an opportunist, Lang replied that he was a man of great moral courage and integrity, but also a pragmatic professional. He was dedicated to opera, which the public rejected; in his search for a way out, he finally hit upon the answer, half accidentally and half by reasoning. The problem was how to continue to write dramatic music and yet appeal to English taste. The dramatic oratorio and masque was the answer. That posterity made this music into quasi-church music was not Handel's fault—but that is another story.

6

As the sixth and final speaker, Bertrand H. Bronson had the difficult task of applying the vague overall topic to the enormous field of letters. He chose to give a special literary meaning to the terms 'man' and 'society'. Bernard N. Schilling summed up the decision this way:

In his treatment, 'man' becomes the man of letters, at first the poet, then mainly the novelist. 'Society' becomes the audience whom he addresses, whose favour he seeks, and rapport with whom he must establish. If there is an economic man, a political man, so also is there a literary man, who bears a certain relationship to the readers whom he addresses. Man, then, is not the subject of literature, but the creator of it, not the subject-matter of Pope's *Essay of Man*, but Pope himself, seeking out the best means whereby to capture and hold the attention of his readers.

What Bronson has done is to see the writer 'from within his works', to see his relationship with his readers, and 'how his point of view, his artistic means, create a certain harmony between him and his readers'.

In his commentary Schilling concentrated on the central issue involved. If the barrier of print deprived the author of what had once been a special sympathetic rapport with his audience, the great eighteenth-century novelists struggled valiantly to overcome their loss. Bronson clearly showed how Richardson, Fielding, and Sterne did achieve a special kind of relationship with a host of readers they would never see. Bronson himself obviously regretted the loss of the older oral tradition, of the precious relationship which had nurtured men like Chaucer and Shakespeare. Yet he allowed a subsequent compensation. So Schilling asked:

Is it not in fact the printed word and its greatly enlarged scope that made possible the complex and variegated attempt to recover a lost mode which Mr Bronson has examined? Are not his eighteenth-century novelists as great as they are, because it was their good fortune to have the printed word at their command, without which they would have suffered a fatal limitation toward their fulfilment?

Again, without bringing charges of descent into mere McLuhanism, wherein method is meaning, we may ask whether what Mr Bronson sees as limitations or impediments to the author are not in fact, as he himself at times implies, gains toward a greater subtlety and a greater enlargement. Thus the difficulty becomes an advantage, calling into play, as it does, new resources, demanding new ironies and suggestive ambiguities. In turn, is not this new uncertainty and duality part of the end to be attained? In noting that Swift would have been inconceivable without the printed word, Mr Bronson seems to concede gains that offset the losses he deplores. In the case of Fielding, however personal and intimate the presentation of himself, a comic distance, a detachment emerges in which author and reader are joined. In *Tristram Shandy* as well, is it not better for Sterne to allow the reader to be puzzled, to come to his own conclusions?

To such far-reaching questions, of course, no answer could be expected in the few minutes remaining. Essentially what Bronson had done was to pose an important problem without professing to have solved it, and the commentators who followed could merely suggest other approaches.

So ended an exciting meeting, which posed many complex and provocative questions for future conferences to examine. Obviously much was left unsolved. Some may wonder whether the plight of the ordinary man in the eighteenth century was quite as bad as some of the speakers implied. In other fields of endeavour, could it have been worse? Or better? Would a widening of scope have changed the picture materially? The questions continue to multiply. What is certain is that eighteenth-century man was not being lulled into complacency by a benevolent, rational society. On the contrary, this was a period of infinitely complex transitions—in the political and commercial worlds, in religion, in the arts—and, we suspect, in those areas of action and conduct unexplored by this symposium.

NOTES

PAGE 2

1 For a fuller discussion of the growth of the electorate in the seventeenth century and its consequences for the politics of the period 1689–1715 see J. H. Plumb, *The Growth of Political Stability in England, 1675–1725* (London, 1967), pp. 34–47.

PAGE 3

1 *Ibid.* pp. 66–97.
2 John Smith (1655–1723) of South Tedworth, Hants. A leading Whig, a friend of the Junto who was a Lord of the Treasury from 1694 to 1702; Chancellor of the Exchequer 1699–1701, 1708–10; Commissioner of the Union with Scotland 1706; Speaker 1705–8. A close friend of Sir Robert Walpole, he sat in parliament 1679–81, 1691–1723. (*Dictionary of National Biography.*) William Bromley (1664–1732) of Bagington, Warwickshire, a leading Tory who was Commissioner of Public Accounts 1696–1705; Speaker 1710–13; Secretary of State 1713–14. M.P. 1689–98, 1701–32. (*Dictionary of National Biography.*)
3 W. A. Speck, 'The Choice of a Speaker in 1705', *Bulletin of the Institute of Historical Research*, XXXVII (1964), 20–35.
4 Camb. Univ. Lib. *C(holmondeley) H(oughton) MSS*, Charles Turner to Robert Walpole, 31 October 1705.
5 The votes of the House of Commons were printed; totals of divisions were given, not names of voters.
6 A seat at Amersham (Bucks.) was under dispute. This is described as a pocket borough of the Drakes (Tories) by Walcott (Robert Walcott, *English Politics in the Early Eighteenth Century* (Oxford, 1956), pp. 13, 40). However, in 1705 party division reared its head. Sir Samuel Garrard, one of the Tory members, afterwards the Lord Mayor of London who invited Sacheverell to preach in 1710, had supported the Tack, and Sir Thomas Webster, an ardent and rich Whig, decided to oppose him. Two polls were taken because Webster insisted that all inhabitants not receiving alms had the right to vote: the Tories maintained only those paying church rates had the right. The two polls were:

	Inhabitants	Ratepayers
Viscount Newhaven (T)	90	58
Sir Samuel Garrard (T)	84	54
Sir Thomas Webster (W)	91	41

The interesting fact here is the very considerable support given to Sir Thomas Webster in a tiny town dominated by the great estate and house of Shardeloes

Notes

which belonged to the Drakes. Doubtless Webster's money helped to strengthen some Whig sentiments, but he also possessed a solid voting base. This is an excellent illustration of the strength of party in a closed borough (see *Hist. MSS Comm.* xv, app. 4, 180), but there are many others.

7 These figures refer to the division on the choice of Speaker: Smith won by 248 to 205. Seymour had led the opposition to Smith.

8 *C(holmondeley) H(oughton) MSS,* John Turner to Robert Walpole, 7 December 1705.

PAGE 5

1 For these and further examples, see J. H. Plumb, *The Growth of Political Stability in England, 1675–1725* (London, 1967), pp. 66–97; L. B. Namier, *The Structure of Politics at the Accession of George III* (2nd ed., London, 1961), pp. 102–4; G. Rudé, *The Crowd in History* (New York, 1964), pp. 47–64.

PAGE 6

1 Plumb, *op. cit.* pp. 78 f. For Buckingham, F. P. and M. M. Verney, *Memoirs of the Verney Family during the Seventeenth Century* (London, 1907), II, 380–8.

PAGE 7

1 For the way votes were carefully scrutinised, see J. H. Plumb, *Sir Robert Walpole* (London, 1960), II, 322.

2 In 1784 Chester cost the Grosvenors £8,500 for food and drink for 3,000 electors: Gervas Huxley, *Lady Elizabeth and the Grosvenors* (London, 1965), pp. 85–6. Essex in 1763 is said to have cost both sides over £30,000: L. B. Namier and J. Brooke, *History of Parliament 1754–90* (London, 1964), I, 4.

PAGE 8

1 L. B. Namier and J. Brooke, *op. cit.* I, 9. At six general elections during this period there were only 37 county contests out of a possible 240.

2 *Ibid.* I *passim.*

3 *C(holmondeley) H(oughton) MSS,* John Wrott to Robert Walpole, 31 May 1710; G. Rudé, *The Crowd in History,* p. 35. He cites riots in South Yorkshire and Nottinghamshire in 1791 and 1798 respectively.

PAGE 9

1 Leon Radzinowitz, *A History of English Criminal Law* (London, 1948), I, 4–5. 'Broadly speaking, in the course of the hundred and sixty years from the Restoration to the death of George III, the number of capital offences had increased by about one hundred and ninety.'

PAGE 10

1 L. W. Hanson, *The Government and the Press* (Oxford, 1936), p. 85. Also, *C(holmondeley) H(oughton) MSS*, 74, folios 12, 13, 64.
2 J. H. Plumb, *Sir Robert Walpole*, II, 142.
3 John Loftis, *The Politics of Drama in Augustan England* (Oxford, 1963), pp. 63–127.

PAGE 11

1 Nicolas Hans, *New Trends in Education in the Eighteenth Century* (London, 1951).
2 G. A. Cranfield, *The Development of the Provincial Newspaper, 1700–1760* (Oxford, 1962), pp. 215–16.
3 *Ibid.* pp. 168–206.

PAGE 12

1 The only copy of this newspaper is in my possession. Many issues contain detailed reports from America, for example 4 August 1768, which prints three and a half columns on riots in Boston; pro-American arguments were printed and so too were the arguments of 'Scrutator', who followed 'the Pennsylvanian Farmer's insidious epistles' and wrote to refute them (4 August 1768). The paper was much more strongly biased towards Wilkes than towards the American colonies, although again the paper was careful to print an occasional satirical thrust at Wilkes himself (e.g. 18 August 1768—the Strutter to J. Wilkes, Esq.). There were at least two debating societies in Liverpool at this time, the Conversation Club and the Debating Society, which concerned themselves with politics, the latter being the more radical. A similar awareness of political issues and widespread public interest in politics existed throughout the West Midlands, particularly Birmingham.
2 Ann Finer and George Savage, *The Selected Letters of Josiah Wedgwood* (London, 1965).
3 R. S. Fitton and A. P. Wadsworth, *The Strutts and the Arkwrights* (Manchester, 1958).
4 G. Rudé, *Wilkes and Liberty* (Oxford, 1962), pp. 220–3. Also 'The Middlesex Electors', *EHR* (1960), pp. 601–17.

PAGE 13

1 J. H. Plumb, *Sir Robert Walpole*, II, 251–67; E. R. Turner, 'The Excise Crisis', *EHR* (1927), pp. 34–57.

PAGE 14

1 Anthony Lincoln, *English Dissent, 1763–1800* (Cambridge, 1938); Eugene Charlton Black, *The Association* (Cambridge, Mass., 1963), pp. 174–212.

Notes

PAGE 16

1 *The Diary of Sylas Neville 1767–1788*, ed. Basil Cozens-Hardy (Oxford, 1950), pp. 90–1, 149. See also Caroline Robbins's pioneer work, *The Eighteenth Century Commonwealthman* (Cambridge, Mass., 1959)

2 Black, *op. cit.* pp. 31–130; H. Butterfield, *George III, Lord North and the People 1779–80* (London, 1949), pp. 229–68.

PAGE 17

1 César de Saussure, *A Foreign View of England in the Reigns of George I and George II* (London, 1902), p. 162.

2 G. Rudé, *The Crowd in History 1730–48*, particularly chapter IV, 'Labour Disputes in Eighteenth-Century England'.

3 Nicolas Hans, *New Trends in Education in the Eighteenth Century* (London, 1951), p. 177.

4 P. S. Foner, *The Complete Writings of Thomas Paine*, ed. P. S. Foner (New York, 1945), II, 910. 'At least one hundred thousand copies of the cheap edition were sold in England, Ireland, and Scotland' (*ibid.* I, xxx).

5 Quoted by James T. Boulton, *The Language of Politics in the Age of Wilkes and Burke* (London, 1963), p. 138. Also M. G. Jones, *Hannah More* (Cambridge, 1952), p. 133, where it is reported that pt II was found 'lurking at the bottom of mines and coalpits'. And A. Temple Patterson, *Radical Leicester* (Leicester, 1959), p. 72.

PAGE 18

1 Of course some rich men stayed loyal to their reformist principles, more it would seem in the provinces than the metropolis. Josiah Wedgwood welcomed the French Revolution, as did Thomas Walker of Manchester to his cost. See Frida Knight, *The Strange Case of T. Walker* (London, 1957).

2 *The American Correspondence of a Bristol Merchant 1766–1776*, ed. G. H. Guttridge (Berkeley, Calif., 1934), p. 6; Namier and Brooke, *History of Parliament 1754–1790*, I, 206–7; W. E. Minchinton, *Politics and the Port of Bristol in the Eighteenth Century* (Bristol, 1963), p. xxxi.

PAGE 19

1 *Wedgwood MSS* (Barlaston). Josiah Wedgwood to Thomas Bentley 7 August 1779. Wedgwood remained unconvinced by those radicals who opposed raising a regiment of militia in Staffordshire in order to free troops for America. 'I am not at present fully convinced by them, that it is better to fall a prey to a foreign enemy rather than defend ourselves under the present ministry. Methinks I would defend the land of my nativity, my family and friends against a foreign foe, where conquest and slavery were inseparable, under any leaders—the best I could get for the moment, and wait for better times to displace an obnoxious minister, and settle domestic affairs, rather

Man Versus Society in Eighteenth-Century Britain

than rigidly say, I'll be saved in my own way and by people of my own choice, or perish and perish my country with me.' I owe this quotation to Mr Neil McKendrick.

PAGE 20

1 For Hannah More, see M. G. Jones, *Hannah More* (Cambridge, 1952). For the growth of working-class literacy, R. K. Webb, *The British Working Class Reader 1790–1848* (London, 1955); Donald Read, *Press and People 1790–1850* (London, 1961).

2 Temple Patterson, *op. cit.* pp. 146–55, 186–8.

PAGE 24

1 For a rich supply of information bearing on the extent of decentralisation and of surrender to private agencies of governmental functions, see: Frederick Clifford, *A History of Private Bill Legislation*, 2 vols. (London, 1885, 1887); E. G. Dowdell, *A Hundred Years of Quarter Sessions. The Government of Middlesex from 1660 to 1760* (Cambridge, 1932); and the series of studies of English local government, beginning in 1906, published by Sidney and Beatrice Webb. See also, for the role of private informers in the detection and prosecution of crime, M. W. Beresford, 'The Common Informer, the Penal Statutes and Economic Regulation', *Economic History Review*, 2nd ser. X (1957), 221–38.

PAGE 26

1 On Robert Walpole's excise scheme, see: Emanuel Leser, *Ein Accisestreit in England*, in a *Festgabe* for J. C. Bluntschli, Heidelberg, 1879, but also published separately; E. R. Turner, 'The Excise Scheme of 1733', *English Historical Review*, XLII (1927), 34–57. For the general history of controversy in England over excises, see Stephen Dowell, *A History of Taxation and Taxes in England* (New York, 1965), reprint of 2nd ed. (London, 1888).

2 Stephen Dowell, *op. cit.* IV, 211–12.

3 Cited by Henry Home, Lord Kames, *Sketches of the History of Man* (Edinburgh, 1774), I, 459.

PAGE 27

1 William Cobbett, ed., *The Parliamentary History of England* (London, 1806–20), XIV, 1318–19.

2 *The Wealth of Nations* [1776], Edwin Cannan, ed. (London, 1925), II, 351–2.

3 *Ibid.* I, 68.

PAGE 29

1 *Thoughts on the Cause of the Present Discontents* [1770], *Works*, Bohn ed. (London, 1854), I, 337.

2 *Thoughts on Civil Liberty* (London, 1765), p. 87.

Notes

3 *Political Register*, J. Almon, ed., II (1768), cited by Simon Maccoby, *English Radicalism, 1762–1785* (London, 1955), p. 84, n. 4.

4 *Political Arithmetick* (1690), *The Economic Writings of Sir William Petty*, Charles Henry Hull, ed. (Cambridge, 1899), I, 274–5.

5 Letters of 1 April 1766, 3 February 1769, *Voltaire's Correspondence*, Theodore Besterman, ed., Geneva, LXI (1961), 3; LXXI (1962), 81.

PAGE 30

1 For the annotation, see *The Writings of Benjamin Franklin*, Albert Henry Smyth, ed. (New York, 1907), X, 239. In a letter to John Ross, 14 May 1768 (*ibid*. V. 132–4), and also in a note on another tract, Franklin made similar remarks. These remarks were responses to British charges that the Americans were using riots as a political weapon against them.

PAGE 31

1 *A Foreign View of England... The Letters of Monsieur César de Saussure to his Family* (New York, 1902), p. 162.

PAGE 33

1 *Les Avocats des Pauvres* (Paris, 1814), is an excellent collection of French charity sermons of the late seventeenth and the eighteenth centuries.

2 A sermon by Thomas Tenison, archbishop of Canterbury, *Concerning Discretion in Giving Alms* (London, 1681), set the tone for a long line of subsequent sermons advocating or justifying prudent restraint in the giving of aid to the poor. William Law, one of the few outstanding Anglican 'enthusiasts' of the eighteenth century, is the only prominent writer of the century that I have found who preached unbounded or 'heroic' charity. But disapproval of unlimited or indiscriminate charity was not, as modern scholars sometimes suggest, an innovation of the Protestant Reformation, or of Protestantism, or of the Post-Reformation period.

3 M. G. Jones, *The Charity School Movement. A Study of Eighteenth Century Puritanism in Action* (Cambridge, 1938), is an informative but mistitled study. The only 'puritanism' involved was 'puritanism' or austerity preached to and for the poor. Annual charity school sermons in London prior to 1729 are conveniently collected in *Twenty-five Sermons Preached at the Anniversary Meetings in...London and Westminster* (London, 1729). The sermons of later years are available only as contemporaneously published separate pamphlets or as reprinted in the collected works of the individual authors.

PAGE 34

1 *The Works of Thomas Secker, LL.D., Late Lord Archbishop of Canterbury* (new ed., Edinburgh, 1792), sermon cxxxii, III, 507.

2 *Fable of the Bees* (1723 and later editions). See F. B. Kaye's edition (Oxford, 1924), entry for 'Charity-Schools' in Kaye's index, II, 459.

3 Bishop Secker's statement of the discipline which the schools should impose on the children is more specific and goes into more detail than any of the other charity school sermons I have seen, but except for the sermon of Bishop Shipley I refer to later it seems to me quite in conformity with the spirit of all of these sermons that I have read. As a significant eighteenth-century document, I present a somewhat lengthy extract here from Secker's sermon: '...particularly humility should be instilled into them with singular care. They should understand, that the lowest of those whom their own parents maintain are for that very reason their superiors; and that no education given as an alms can be a ground for thinking highly of themselves. Their usage in all respects should be answerable to such lessons. Cleanliness should be required of them, as far as ever their employments allow it; but no extraordinary provision should be made for it, nor the least affectation of nicety be tolerated in either sex. Their clothes should be no better, if so good, as they may hope to wear all the rest of their lives; no gaiety of colour, no trifling ornaments permitted; nor any distinction between them and other children in which they can possibly be tempted to take pleasure. If they are fed, their food should be of the coarsest sort, and not more than enough. If they are lodged, it should be in a manner that is suitable to every thing else. For, besides that frugality is a most important branch of faithfulness in the management of charities, *it is good that they should bear the yoke in their youth* (Lamentations, iii. 27), be inured to the treatment they must expect to receive; and wrong-judged indulgence is the greatest cruelty that can be exercised towards them.' (Sermon cxxxii, *Works*, III, 505.)

PAGE 35

1 *A Sermon Preached [at] the Yearly Meeting of the Children Educated in the Charity-Schools in the Cities of London and Westminster* (London, 1777). Also in Jonathan Shipley, *Works* (London, 1792), II, 331 ff., where see especially II, 338–9, 350–5.

2 'Of Public Spirit in Regard to Public Works' [1736], ll. 45–8, 'Second Version', *The Poetical Works of Richard Savage*, Clarence Tracy, ed. (Cambridge, 1962), p. 226.

PAGE 36

1 'Liberty' (1735–6), part v, ll. 5–7, *The Complete Poetical Works of James Thomson*, J. L. Robertson, ed. (London, 1908), p. 392. Thomson is here thanking the Goddess of Liberty for her special patronage of Britain.

2 19 Geo. II, c. 21 [1746], *Statutes at Large*, London, X (1811), 216.

PAGE 37

1 *A Journey to the Western Isles of Scotland* [1775], R. W. Chapman, ed. (London, 1924), p. 85.

2 *Joseph Andrews* (Scholartis Press ed., London, 1929), p. 289.

Notes

3 *Reflections on Various Subjects Relating to Arts and Commerce* (London, 1752), pp. 72–3.

PAGE 39

1 *History of the Criminal Law of England* (London, 1883), I, 470.
2 See Charles Reith, *The Police Idea* (London, 1938), p. 10. For the period after 1750 the major authority on most aspects of English criminal law is now the multi-volume work of Leon Radzinowicz, *A History of English Criminal Law and its Administration from 1750*, 3 vols. (London, 1948–56).
3 Cited by Richard Burn, *The Justice of the Peace* (7th ed., London, 1762), II, 51. On the later history of the game laws, see Chester Kirby, 'English Game Law Reform', *Essays in Modern English History in Honor of William Cortez Abbott* (Cambridge, Mass., 1941), pp. 345–80.

PAGE 40

1 For the history of 'benefit of clergy', see Stephen, *History of the Criminal Law of England*, vol. I passim.

PAGE 41

1 See F. Iremonger, *William Temple Archbishop of Canterbury, His Life and Letters* (London, 1948, pp. 438–9), for the text of Keynes's letter.
2 *A Sermon against Clipping* (London, 1694), pp. 23–4, 28–9.

PAGE 42

1 *The Idler*, no. 22, 16 September 1758 and no. 38, 6 January 1759, reprinted in *The British Essayists* (London), XXXIII (1823), 70–3, 122–6. For the efforts of a voluntary agency to alleviate the conditions of those imprisoned for debt, see James Neild, *An Account of the Rise, Progress, and Present State, of the Society for the Discharge and Relief of Persons Imprisoned for Small Debts* (London, 1802). Neild was an officer of this society from 1773 on.

PAGE 43

1 The severity of the treatment of defaulters on debt payment was often as great in ancient Rome, in the Middle Ages, and in post-Reformation Catholic countries as in eighteenth-century England. Cf. Thorsten Sellin's Foreword to Georg Rusche and Otto Kirchheimer, *Punishment and Social Structure* (New York, 1939), p. vi: 'The sanguinary punishments and tortures of old are no evidence of bloodthirstiness or sadism on the part of those who used them. They rather testify to the fact that those who designed them could conceive of no better, that is, more efficient, way of securing protection for the social values which they treasured.'

PAGE 44

1 *The History of the Poor Laws* (London, 1764), p. 120.

PAGE 45

1 'An Essay towards Preventing the Ruin of Great Britain' (1721), in *The Works of George Berkeley*, A. C. Fraser, ed. (Oxford, 1871), vol. III.

PAGE 46

1 *Ibid.* III, 198.
2 *Our Eminent Friend Edmund Burke* (New Haven, 1949), p. 164.

PAGE 47

1 On John Howard's heroic career as prison reformer, see: John Aikin, *A View of the Character and Public Services of the late John Howard, Esq.* (London, 1792); William A. Guy, 'John Howard's True Place in History', *Journal of the Royal Statistical Association*, XXXVIII (1875), 430–7; D. L. Howard, *John Howard; Prison Reformer* (London, 1958).

PAGE 48

1 *The Equality of Mankind* [1765], new ed. (London, 1799), ll. 295–302.

PAGE 49

1 Few copies of the 1775 edition of his lecture seem to be extant. The 1793 edition, with a new title, is reprinted in M. Beer, ed., *The Pioneers of Land Reform* (New York, 1920), pp. 5–16. For an account of Thomas Spence, see Olive D. Rudkin, *Thomas Spence and his Connections* (London, 1927).
2 *The Fool of Quality* [1767], reprint, London, n.d. (*c.* 1925), p. 346.
3 *Works* (London, 1792), I, 308.

PAGE 51

1 I am relying here mostly on G. E. Fussell, *The English Rural Labourer, His Home, Furniture, Clothing & Food from Tudor to Victorian Times* (London, 1949), ch. V, 'Cottages'. Morland's picture is reproduced on the page opposite p. 65.

PAGE 52

1 See, for example, *Magna Britannia Notitia: Or, The Present State of Great Britain* (London, 1723), p. 189; (1737), p. 177.

PAGE 53

1 C. B. A. Behrens, in a review of two books on the French aristocracy under the *Ancien Régime*, *The New York Review of Books*, 6 October 1966, p. 16.

PAGE 55

1 William Law, *Three Letters to the Bishop of Bangor*, J. O. Nash and C. Gore, eds. (Edinburgh, 1909), p. 74.

Notes

2 Mark Pattison, *Essays* (Oxford, 1889), II, 45.
3 Lord Chesterfield, *Letters*, 8 January 1750.

PAGE 56

1 In two critical divisions, twenty-four out of the twenty-five bishops who voted supported Walpole, and each time the government won by one vote.
2 Cf. *The Life of Zachary Pearce*, in *The Lives of Dr Edward Pocock, of Dr Zachary Pearce, and of Dr Thomas Newton, and of the Rev. Philip Skelton* (London, 1816), II, 392, 397.

PAGE 58

1 Edmund Pyle, *Memoirs of a Royal Chaplain* (London, 1905), pp. 305, 350, 126.
2 Quoted in J. H. Overton and F. Relton, *A History of the English Church* (London, 1906), VI, 160.
3 *Letters from a late Eminent Prelate* (Kidderminster, 1808; London, 1809), VI, 16. Cf. Pyle, *op. cit.* p. 207.
4 Cf. Pyle, *op. cit.* p. 218.

PAGE 59

1 Pyle, *op. cit.* p. 178.
2 *Ibid.* p. 266.
3 Edward F. Carpenter (ed.), *A House of Kings* (London, 1966), p. 211. The dean was Zachary Pearce.

PAGE 60

1 Cf. *Dictionary of National Biography*. For the similar pattern in the career of John Hoadly (son of Benjamin) see Pyle, *op. cit.* pp. 268–9.

PAGE 61

1 This rumour was generally accepted at the time. It has since been challenged and disproved (cf. Norman Sykes, in *Theology*, XXXIII, 1936). Its very prevalence is the best indication that it was plausible to attribute this mood of pessimism to a distinguished churchman; and it was undoubtedly in keeping with certain of Butler's comments of unquestioned authenticity.
2 Cf. Benjamin Hoadly, *A Preservative Against the Principles and Practice of the Non-jurors* (London, 1716).
3 William Wake, *The Authority of Christian Princes over their Ecclesiastical Synods Asserted* (London, 1697), p. 10.
4 *Ibid.* p. 42.
5 William Wake, *The State of the Church and Clergy of England* (London, 1703), p. xii.

PAGE 62

1 Robert Lowth, *A Letter to the Right Reverend Author of the Divine Legation of Moses* (2nd ed., 1765), pp. 42–4.
2 George Crabbe, *The Village*.
3 Boswell, *Life of Samuel Johnson*, ed. Hill-Powell (Oxford, 1934), II, 474 (26 March 1776).

PAGE 63

1 James Woodforde, *The Diary of a Country Parson* (World's Classics ed., 1949), pp. 51, 52, 128, 129, 173, 262, 289.

PAGE 64

1 R. Philip, *Life and Times of the Rev. George Whitefield* (London, 1837), p. 195.
2 *The Lives of Dr Edward Pocock, of Dr Zachary Pearce, of Dr Thomas Newton, and of the Rev. Philip Skelton* (London, 1816), I, 386.

PAGE 65

1 B.M. Add. MSS 33069, folio 469. Quoted by Norman Sykes, *Church and State in England in the XVIIIth Century* (London, 1934), p. 280.
2 John Wesley, *Journal*, ed. Nehemiah Curnock (London, 1938), I, 469.
3 Preface to *Hymns and Sacred Poems* (1739), *The Works of the Rev. John Wesley* (ed. by John Emory, New York, 1850), VII, 593.

PAGE 66

1 *The Works of the Rev. A. M. Toplady* (London, 1825), I, 20, 77, 79.

PAGE 67

1 John Flavel, *The Touchstone of Sincerity* (London, 1698), p. 16; 2nd American ed. (New York: n.d., p. 16).
2 William Wilberforce, *A Practical View of the Prevailing Religious System of Professed Christians* (London, 1797), p. 309.
3 *Ibid.* p. 304.
4 Mary Milner, *The Life of Isaac Milner* (London, 1842), p. 77.

PAGE 68

1 Edmund Burke, *Reflections on the French Revolution*, in *Works* (London, 1792), III, 66.
2 *Ibid.* III, 129.

PAGE 69

1 *Ibid.* III, 139.
2 *Ibid.* III, 144.

Notes

PAGE 70

1 Cf. R. and M. Wittkower, *Born under Saturn* (London and New York, 1963), p. 71; also for the following, *passim*.
2 *Ibid.* p. 228.

PAGE 71

1 For this and the following passages, cf. pp. 29–37 of Richardson's *Essay*.

PAGE 73

1 John Fleming, *Robert Adam and his Circle* (Harvard University Press, 1962), p. 173.
2 *Ibid.* p. 114.
3 James Northcote, *The Life of Sir Joshua Reynolds* (London, 1818), I, 103.
4 Jean Rouquet, *The Present State of the Arts in England* (London, 1755). Pepys, who knew Lely well, entered into his Diary in 1666: '...a mighty proud man he is, and full of state.'
5 *Op. cit.*

PAGE 74

1 John Pye, *Patronage of British Art, An Historical Sketch* (London, 1845), p. 24, reprints this anecdote from Strype's *Annals*.
2 Jonathan Richardson, *An Essay on the Theory of Painting* (London, 1715), pp. 23 f.

PAGE 75

1 This problem has been discussed, among others, by Edgar Wind (*Journal of the Warburg Institute*, II (1938–9), 182 ff.), Charles Mitchell (*Burlington Magazine*, LXXX (1942), 35 ff.) and Ernst Gombrich (*ibid.* pp. 40 ff.).

PAGE 76

1 Pye, *op. cit.* p. 43, note 43.
2 For this and the following, cf. Hogarth's autobiographical sketch in John Ireland and John Nichols, *Hogarth's Works*, Edinburgh and London (n.d.), III, pp. 64 f.
3 *Ibid. loc. cit.*

PAGE 77

1 For the following, cf. Nikolaus Pevsner, *Academies of Art Past and Present* (Cambridge, 1940); W. T. Whitley, *Artists and their Friends in England 1700–1799* (Cambridge, 1928), I, 7 ff.

PAGE 78

1 Cf. Hogarth's spirited account, in Ireland–Nichols, *op. cit.* III, 57.
2 *Op. cit.* p. 23.

3 *The Plan of an Academy for the better Cultivation, Improvement, and Encouragement, of Painting, Sculpture, Architecture...; the Abstract of a Royal Charter as proposed for Establishing the same;...* (London, 1755). An extract from the Introduction of this pamphlet in Pye, *op. cit.* p. 78; also in Charles Robert Leslie and Tom Taylor, *Life and Times of Sir Joshua Reynolds* (London, 1865), I, 131 ff. The authors attribute the text of the Introduction to Reynolds; this seems to me doubtful, since some of the opinions expressed in it are clearly contrary to Reynolds's convictions.

PAGE 79

1 The painter Francis Hayman signed as chairman of the committee. Among its twenty-five members were famous names, e.g. Roubiliac, Thomas Hudson, Samuel Scott, Isaac Ware, Gavin Hamilton, Thomas Sandby, etc.
2 Ireland–Nichols, *op. cit.* III, 59.

PAGE 80

1 For the failure of the negotiations, cf. Whitley, *op. cit.* I, 158 f.
2 A detailed account in Pye, *op. cit.* pp. 87 ff.
3 The minutes of their meetings are summarised in Pye, p. 92, and more explicitly published in *The Walpole Society*, VI (1917–18), 116 ff.
4 Founded in 1754, with Lord Folkestone as President. I am indebted to Professor James L. Clifford for directing my attention to the importance of Samuel Johnson's involvement in the affairs of these artists.
5 These artists refused to exhibit again under the control of the Society for the Encouragement of the Arts, but a less distinguished minority seceded and continued for some time to exhibit in the great room of the Society. For further details regarding the important events of 1761, cf. Pye, *op. cit.* pp. 97 ff., and William Sandby, *The History of the Royal Academy of Arts* (London, 1862), pp. 34 f.

PAGE 81

1 The entire preface is printed in James Northcote, *Memoirs of Sir Joshua Reynolds, Knt* (London, 1813), pp. 55 ff. (with caption: 'Written by Dr Johnson'); Pye, *op. cit.* pp. 106 ff.; Sandby, *op. cit.* I, 37 f. See also Leslie and Taylor, *op. cit.* I, 203; and Allen T. Hazen, *Samuel Johnson's Prefaces and Dedications* (New Haven, 1937), pp. 200–5.
2 Ireland–Nichols, *op. cit.* III, 30.

PAGE 82

1 For Boydell, cf. Monkhouse's article in *DNB* and T. S. R. Boase, in *Journal of the Warburg and Courtauld Institutes*, X (1947), 94 ff.; also Pye, *op. cit.* pp. 248 ff.

Notes

2 Northcote, Reynolds's pupil, wrote about Boydell that he 'did more for the advancement of the arts in England than the whole mass of nobility put together. He paid me more nobly than any other person has done; and his memory I shall ever hold in reverence'; cf. Pye, *op. cit.* p. 249.

PAGE 83

1 The toast was proposed by Burke, who handed to the President, Reynolds, the following note: 'This end of the table, at which as there are many admirers of the art there are many friends of yours, wish to drink to an English tradesman who patronizes the art better than the Grand Monarque of France.' Cf. Leslie and Taylor, *op. cit.* II, 532 f.

PAGE 86

1 Romain Rolland, *Haendel* (Paris, 1910); English translation, London, 1916.

PAGE 87

1 Ernst Hermann Meyer, *English Chamber Music* (London, 1951).

PAGE 88

1 Percy A. Scholes, *The Puritans and Music* (London, 1934).

PAGE 89

1 See chapters V and VI in Ernest Walker, *A History of Music in England*, 3rd edition, revised and enlarged by J. A. Westrup (Oxford, 1952).

PAGE 91

1 See Steele's and Addison's articles in the *Tatler* and *Spectator*, 1709–12.

PAGE 93

1 To mention one example, in the seventeenth to eighteenth centuries Venice had an opera theatre in practically every parish. These theatres, named after the patron saint of the parish, at one time numbered sixteen!

PAGE 99

1 See E. Stanley Roper 'The Chapels Royal and their Music', in *Proceedings of the Royal Musical Association* (1928); Cart de Lafontaine, *The King's Musick* (London, 1909).
2 Charles Avison's *An Essay on Musical Expression* appeared in 1752, Daniel Webb's *Observations on the Correspondence between Poetry and Music* in 1769, and the two great histories of Hawkins and Burney in 1776 (the latter finished in 1789).

PAGE 100

1 Hubert Langley, *Doctor Arne* (Cambridge, 1938).
2 See Edward M. Gagey, *Ballad Opera* (New York, 1937).

PAGE 102

1 Lord Kames [Henry Home], *Elements of Criticism*, XVIII, 2.
2 Geoffrey Chaucer, 'General Prologue', *Canterbury Tales*, ll. 725–33.
3 John Keats, 'In a Drear-nighted December' [early printed version], ll. 21–4.

PAGE 106

1 John Whiteside Saunders, *The Profession of English Letters* (London, 1964), p. 93.

PAGE 107

1 *Ibid.* p. 114.

PAGE 109

1 Matthew Prior, *Hans Carvel*, ll. 21–42.
2 Alexander Pope, *Ode for Musick, on St Cecilia's Day*, l. 1.
3 Pope, *An Essay on Man*, I, ll. 1–2.

PAGE 110

1 Pope, *The Second Epistle of the Second Book of Horace*, ll. 76–9.

PAGE 111

1 *Ibid.* ll. 108–9.
2 Pope, *Epilogue to the Satires*, Dialogue II, ll. 197–200, 208–9.

PAGE 112

1 *Ibid.* ll. 246–7.

PAGE 114

1 *The Letters of Samuel Johnson*, ed. R. W. Chapman (1952), II, 228 [27 October 1777].
2 J. W. Saunders, *op. cit.* pp. 104–5.

PAGE 115

1 *Alice in Wonderland*, chapter VI.
2 Daniel Defoe, *Robinson Crusoe*.

PAGE 116

1 *Alice in Wonderland*, chapter VI.
2 Ian Watt, *The Rise of the Novel* (Berkeley, 1964), p. 119.

Notes

PAGE 117

1 *Gulliver's Travels*, part I, chapter 1, 2nd paragraph.

PAGE 120

1 Quoted by E. L. McAdam, Jr, in *Yale Review*, 2nd ser. XXXVIII (1948), 304–5.

PAGE 122

1 *Tom Jones*, book VII, chapter 12. Cf. *Troilus and Criseyde*, book III, ll. 575 ff. and I, ll. 492 ff.

PAGE 123

1 *Tristram Shandy*, book II, chapter 11.

PAGE 125

1 *Ibid.* book I, chapter 21.

PAGE 127

1 *Boswell's Life of Johnson*, II, 449 [20 March 1776].

PAGE 129

1 *Tristram Shandy*, book III, chapter 37.
2 Report of a lecture at Stanford University, in the *San Francisco Chronicle* (*San Francisco Sunday Examiner and Chronicle*), 15 May 1966, 'This World' Supplement, p. 41.

PAGE 130

1 Quoted in Marshall McLuhan, *Understanding Media* (New York: McGraw-Hill, paperback ed., 1965), p. 53.

PAGE 131

1 Cf. Stendhal, *Le Rouge et le Noir*, epigraph to part I, chapter 13: 'Un roman: c'est un miroir qu'on promène le long d'un chemin.' (Saint-Réal.)
2 Wayne Booth, *The Rhetoric of Fiction* (Chicago, 1961), pp. 378–84.

PAGE 138

1 Walt Whitman Rostow, *The Stages of Economic Growth* (Cambridge, 1960).

PAGE 139

1 'Changes in English Fertility and Mortality, 1781–1850', *Economic History Review*, XI (August, 1958), 52–70; and 'Population Change in England as an Economic Variable, 1700–1850', paper delivered to the American Historical Association, Chicago, 1962.

Man Versus Society in Eighteenth-Century Britain

PAGE 140

1 James Boswell, *Life of Johnson*, ed. Hill-Powell, III, 406 [10 October 1779];
Raymond W. Postgate, *That Devil Wilkes* (New York, 1929), pp. 230–5.

PAGE 142

1 Cf. Wittkower's discussion, pp. 74–5.

Throughout the Commentary the editor has had valuable help from Dr
J. Jean Hecht, and from the following commentators: Harvey C. Mansfield,
Jr (Harvard University), Albert H. Imlah (Tufts University), Lewis A. Dralle
(University of Wichita, Kansas), Ronald H. Paulson (Johns Hopkins University), Donald Grout (Cornell University), Bernard N. Schilling (Rochester
University).

INDEX

Abel, Karl Friedrich (1723–87), 99
Academy of Ancient Music, 99
Adam, Robert (1728–92), 73
Addison, Joseph (1672–1719), 110, 146, 148, 165
administration, public, 23–5
Albemarle, William Anne Keppel, 2nd earl of (1702–54), 73
Alice in Wonderland, 115, 116
America, 1, 14, 15, 154; war of independence, 13, 18, 19, 46
Amersham, Bucks., 3, 152
Anacharsis (sixth century B.C.), 36
Anne, queen of England (1665–1714), 2, 4, 109, 110
Ariosti Attilio (1666–1740), 99
Arne, Thomas Augustine (1710–78), 100
Ashbourne, Derbyshire, 62
Ashton, Thomas S., 133
Athelstan, king of the English (d. 940), 41
Atterbury, Francis, bishop of Rochester (1662–1732), 61
Avison, Charles (1709–70), 99

Bach, Johann Sebastian (1685–1750), 87, 88, 89, 96, 146
Bach, John Christian (1735–82), 99
Bacon, Francis (1561–1626), 78
Bangorian controversy, 141
Bath, 99
Battishill, Jonathan (1738–1801), 100
Beckford, William (1709–70), 18
Bedfordshire, 57
Bedingfield, 8
Beethoven, Ludwig van (1770–1827), 92, 99
Bellow, Saul, 129
Bentley, Thomas (1731–80), 12, 155
Berkeley, George, bishop of Cloyne (1685–1753), 45
Bible, Handel's use of, 87, 89, 96–7
Biggs, William (c. 1800–81), 19
Birmingham, 154
bishoprics, 57, 141
bishops, Hanoverian, basis of promotion of, 57, 58; moral standards, concern for, 63; political activities of, 56–8, 161

Blake, William (1757–1827), 70
Bolingbroke, Henry St John, Viscount (1678–1751), 6
Bononcini, Giovanni (1670–1747), 99
Booth, Wayne C. *The Rhetoric of Fiction*, 131
Boswell, James (1740–95), 62, 127
Bourdaloue, Louis (1632–1704), 33
Boyce, William (1710–79), 100
Boydell, John (1719–1804), 82–3, 165
Brade, William (c. 1560–1630), 87
bribery, 5 ff.
Bristol, 2, 12, 18, 57
Britain, identity discussed, 135
Broadwood & Sons, 99
Bromley, William (1664–1732), 3, 152
Brooke, Henry (1703?–83), *Fool of Quality*, 49
Brower [Brouwer], Adriaen (1605?–38), 70
Brown, John (1715–66), *Thoughts on Civil Liberty*, 29
Buckingham, 6, 153
Burgh, James (1714–75), 48
Burke, Edmund (1729–97), vii, 14, 18; and American grievances, 15; on *Beggar's Opera*, 100; conservatism, 47; definition of 'people', 29; distrust of theories, 68; economic reform bill, 46; organic view of society, 68–9; toasts Boydell, 165; views man as basically religious, 68–9
Burleigh, William Cecil, 1st Baron (1520–98), 104
Burn, Richard (1709–85), 44
Burney, Charles (1726–1814), 95, 99, 165
Burrards, family of, at Lymington, 5
Bute, John Stuart, 3rd earl of (1713–92), 26
Butler, Joseph, bishop of Durham (1692–1752), 34, 60–1, 161; *Analogy*, 60

Calvin, John (1509–64), attitude towards music, 88
Cambridge, 10, 11, 67, 140, 148
Canterbury, 57, 60
Caravaggio, Michelangelo Amerighi da (1565–1609), 70
Cartwright, John (1740–1824), 12, 17
Caryl, Lynford (c. 1708–81), 58

Index

Index

Index

Kent, 8

Keynes, John Maynard, 1st Baron (1883–1946), 41

King's Lynn, Norfolk, 3, 10

Kneller, Sir Godfrey (1646–1723), 73, 77, 145

Krause, John T. 139

laissez faire, 22–3, 46

Lancashire, 16, 139

Last Determinations Act, 1729, 7

law, canon, 40; capital punishment, 40–1, 153; criminal, 37–9; equality before the, 35–40; game, 39–40; imprisonment for debts, 41–3, 159; poor, 43–6

Law, William (1686–1761), 55, 141–2, 157

Leicester corporation, 20

Leighs, family of, at Lyme, 5

Lely, Sir Peter (1618–80), 73, 163

Leonardo da Vinci (1452–1519), 85

letter writing, 112–14, 119, 121

Lichfield, Staffs., 60

Linley, Thomas, Sr. (1732–95), 100

literacy, evidences of, 17, 31; fear of, 18, 30–1; growth of, 1, 10–12, 156; growth of questioned, 140

Liverpool, 11, 12, 154; *Liverpool Chronicle*, 11; Debating Society, 15

Locke, John (1632–1704), 55

Loeillet, Jean-Baptiste [John], (1680–1730), 99

London, bishop of, 96, *see* Gibson

London, bishops residing in, 57; *Evening Post*, 10; in literary works, 108–9, 117; musical life of, 94, 99; radicalism in, 16–17; stage, 10

Lords, House of, role of bishops in, 56

Louis XIV, king of France (1638–1715), 77, 89

Lowth, Robert, bishop of London (1710–87), 62

Macclesfield, Thomas Parker, 1st earl of (1666?–1732), 64

McLuhan, Marshall, 130, 150

Manchester, 99, 140

Mandeville, Bernard (1670–1733), 34

Mansfield, Harvey C., Jr., 135–7, 168

Mansfield, William Murray, 1st earl of (1705–93), 140

Marlborough, John Churchill, 1st duke of (1650–1722), 4

Massillon, Jean Baptiste (1663–1742), 33

Mathias, Thomas James (1754?–1835), 17

Mendip Hills, Somerset, 68

Middlesex, mobs, 5; Wilkes election, 11, 12, 13

Milner, Isaac (1750–1820), 67

Milton, John (1608–74), 78, 88, 107

mob violence, 5, 13, 30, 134

Montagu, Lady Mary Wortley (1689–1762) 113

Montesquieu, Charles Louis de Secondat, Baron de (1689–1755), 137

Monteverdi, Claudio (1567–1643), 88

Mor, Antonio (*c.* 1512–75), 73

More, Hannah (1745–1833), 19, 55, 67–8, 156

More, Sir Thomas (1478–1535), *Utopia*, 53

Morland, George (1763–1804), 50, 160

Mozart, Wolfgang Amadeus (1756–91), 97, 100

Namier, Sir Lewis B. (1888–1960), 12, 13

Napoleon I (1769–1821), 19

Neville, Sylas (1741–1840), 15–16

Newcastle, 12, 48, 57

Newcastle, Thomas Pelham-Holles, 1st duke of (1693–1768), discipline of bishops, 56–7; personal religion, 64–5; as political manipulator, 14–15, 55, 58

Newhaven, William Cheyne, 2nd Viscount (1657–1728), 152

Newton, Sir Isaac (1642–1727), 55, 78

Newton, Thomas, bishop of Bristol (1704–82), 58

Nietzsche, Friedrich Wilhelm (1844–1900), 92

Norfolk militia, 8

North, Brownlow, bishop of Winchester (1741–1820), 60

North, Frederick, 8th Baron (1732–92), 13, 15, 18–19, 60

Northampton Mercury, 11

Northcote, James (1746–1831), 73, 77, 82, 165

Norwich, 2, 3; *Norwich Mercury*, 11

Nottinghamshire, 153

novel, rise of, 114 ff.

O'Hara, John, *Pal Joey*, 130

oligarchy, development of, 1, 9, 20, 137

Index

opera, ballad, 100, 147; characteristics of, 90–3; English opposition to, 88, 90–1, 145; Handel and, 94, 95, 101; Italian, 94, 95, 101, 146, 147

oral tradition in literature, 102, 103, 105, 122, 129

oratorio, 95 ff.

Oxford, 10, 11, 57, 66, 140, 148

Paine, Thomas (1737–1809), 18, 19; *Rights of Man*, 12, 16, 17, 155

Painter–Stainers Company, 75

Paley, William (1743–1805), 62

Pares, Thomas (*fl.* 1800–35), 19

Parliament, Acts of, 1, 2, 5, 7, 8, 13, 20, 26, 36, 46, 47; Addresses to 13–14; reform of, 16

Parrott, Richard, of Hawkesbury (*fl.* mid eighteenth cent.), 37

party system, decline of, 138

Patrick, Simon, bishop of Chichester (1626–1707), 141–2

patriotism, effects of, 14, 17, 18–19

patronage, of artists, 75 ff. 144; of churchmen, 56 ff.; in politics, 6 *passim*; of writers, 109–10

Paulson, Ronald H. 71, 142–4, 168

Pearce, Zachary, bishop of Rochester (1690–1774), 59, 64, 161

Pepusch, John Christopher (1667–1752), 100

Pepys, Samuel (1633–1703), 163

periods, historical, concept of, 135–6

Petty, Sir William (1623–87), 29

Pitt, William, 1st earl of Chatham (1708–78), vii, 12, 15

Pitt, William (1759–1806), 19

Playford, John (1623–86), 88

pluralism, ecclesiastical, 59–60

Political Register, 29

Pompey the Little, novel by Francis Coventry (1751), 126

Pope, Alexander (1688–1744), vii, 107, 112; *Dunciad*, 93; *Epilogue to the Satires*, 111, 112; *Essay on Man*, 109, 149; Horatian imitations, 110, 111; *St Cecilia Ode*, 109

portrait-painter's atelier, functioning of, 144–5

prebendaries, competition for, 58–9

press-gang, 46

Price, Richard (1723–91), 12, 17

Priestley, Joseph (1733–1804), 12, 17

printing, its effect upon literature, 103 ff, 149–50

Prior, Matthew (1664–1721), 107, 108, 109, 110; *Hans Carvel*, 108–9

prison reform, 47

privacy, invasion of, 25–7

Profane Oaths Act of 1746, 36

property, importance of, 9, 17, 18, 140

provincial press, 11

Punch and Judy shows, 10

Purcell, Henry (1659–95), 89, 94, 146; *Dido and Aeneas*, 93–4; his work characterised, 90

Puritans, attitude towards music, 88; attitude towards reading, 140

Pye, John (1782–1874), *Patronage of British Art*, 78

Pyle, Edmund (1702–76), *Memoirs*, 59

Quantz, Johann Joachim (1697–1773), 99

Radicalism, 15–19, 48–50, 137, 138

Ramsay, Allan (1713–84), 72–3

Raphael Santi (1483–1520), 143

Rashleighs, family of, at Fowey, 5

Reform Bill of 1832, 20

Religious experience, absence of in some clergymen, 62–3; among Evangelicals, 66; re-emergence of, 54; in Wesley's revival, 65

Revolution of 1688, 2, 9, 22, 27, 136–7

Reynolds, Frances (1729–1807), 73

Reynolds, Sir Joshua (1723–92), vii, 83, 164; carriage of, 73; heroicising English middle class, 107, 142, 143; Hogarth, contrasted to, 82, 142–4; popularity of, 75; price of portraits, 145; and Royal Academy, 79, 81; social position of, 72, 73, 77

Richardson, Jonathan, the elder (1665–1745), 71, 72, 74, 76, 83, 84

Richardson, Samuel (1689–1761), 118, 123, 149; *Clarissa*, 119, 120, 121; fictional technique of, 118–21, 122

riots, 5, 30, 153, 154, 157

Robin Hood debating society, 17

Rockingham, Charles Watson-Wentworth, 2nd marquess of (1730–82), 15, 26

Rolland, Romain (1866–1944), 86

Ross, John [of Phila.] (1714–76), 157

Rostow, Walt Whitman, 138

Roubiliac, Louis François (1695?–1762), 164

Rouquet, André (1701–58), 73

Rousseau, Jean Jacques (1712–78), 49

Royal Academy, formation of, 77–84; membership in, 144

173

Index

Index

IN THE NORTON LIBRARY

Gash, Norman. *Politics in the Age of Peel.* N564

Gatzke, Hans W. *Stresemann and the Rearmament of Germany.* N486

Gay, Peter. *The Party of Humanity: Essays in the French Enlightenment.* N607

Graves, Robert and Alan Hodge. *The Long Week-end: A Social History of Great Britain, 1918–1939.* N217

Greene, Jack P. *The Quest for Power: The Lower Houses of Assembly in the Southern Royal Colonies, 1689–1776.* N591

Halperin, S. William. *Germany Tried Democracy.* N280

Hamilton, Holman. *Prologue to Conflict.* N345

Haring, C. H. *Empire in Brazil.* N386

Haskins, Charles Homer. *The Normans in European History.* N342

Hill, Christopher. *The Century of Revolution 1603–1714.* N365

Holmes, George. *The Later Middle Ages, 1272–1485.* N363

Huizinga, Jan. *In the Shadow of Tomorrow.* N484

Jolliffe, J. E. A. *The Constitutional History of Medieval England.* N417

Keir, David Lindsay. *The Constitutional History of Modern Britain Since 1485.* N405

Kendall, Paul Murray. *The Yorkist Age.* N558

Kendall, Paul Murray (editor) *Richard III: The Great Debate.* N310

Kolko, Gabriel. *Railroads and Regulation, 1877–1916.* N531

Lamar, Howard Roberts. *The Far Southwest, 1846–1912.* N522

Leach, Douglass E. *Flintlock and Tomahawk: New England in King Philip's War.* N340

McFeely, William S. *Yankee Stepfather: General O.O. Howard and the Freedmen.* N537

Madison, James. *Notes of Debates in the Federal Convention of 1787.* N485

Magrath, C. Peter. *Yazoo: The Case of Fletcher v. Peck.* N418

Marwick, Arthur. *The Deluge: British Society and the First World War.* N523

Mattingly, Harold. *The Man in the Roman Street.* N337

Mattingly, Harold. *Roman Imperial Civilization.* N572

May, Arthur J. *The Hapsburg Monarchy: 1867–1914.* N460

Mosse, Claude. *The Ancient World at Work.* N540

Neale, J. E. *Elizabeth I and Her Parliaments,* 2 vols. N359a & N359b

Noggle, Burl. *Teapot Dome: Oil and Politics in the 1920's.* N297

North, Douglass C. *The Economic Growth of the United States 1790–1860.* N346

Ogilvie, R. M. *The Romans and Their Gods in the Age of Augustus.* N543

Pelling, Henry. *Modern Britain, 1885–1955.* N368

Pirenne, Henri. *Early Democracies in the Low Countries.* N565

Pollack, Norman. *The Populist Response to Industrial America.* N295

Quirk, Robert E. *The Mexican Revolution, 1914–1915.* N507

Read, Conyers. *The Tudors.* N129

Remini, Robert V. *Martin Van Buren and the Making of the Democratic Party.* N527

Ritcheson, Charles. *Aftermath of Revolution: British Policy Toward the United States, 1783–1795.* N553

Robson, Eric. *The American Revolution, 1763–1783.* N382

Roth, Cecil. *The Spanish Inquisition.* N255

Rowse, A. L. *Appeasement.* N139

Ruiz, Ramon Eduardo. *Cuba: The Making of a Revolution.* N513

Sarton, George. *A History of Science, I: Ancient Science Through the Golden Age of Greece.* N525

Sarton, George. *A History of Science, II: Hellenistic Science and Culture in the Last Three Centuries B.C.* N526

Seton-Watson, R. W. *Disraeli, Gladstone, and the Eastern Question.* N594

Smith, Abbot E. *Colonists in Bondage: White Servitude and Convict Labor in America, 1607–1776.* N592

Sontag, Raymond J. *Germany and England: Background of Conflict, 1848–1894.* N180

Spanier, John W. *The Truman-MacArthur Controversy and the Korean War.* N279

Stansky, Peter and William Abrahams. *Journey to the Frontier: Two Roads to the Spanish Civil War.* N509

Tan, Chester C. *The Boxer Catastrophe.* N575

Tarbell, Ida M. *History of the Standard Oil Company.* N496

Taylor, A. J. P. *Germany's First Bid for Colonies, 1884–1885.* N530

Thompson, J. M. *Louis Napoleon and the Second Empire.* N403

Tolles, Frederick B. *Meeting House and Counting House.* N211

Tourtellot, Arthur Bernon. *Lexington and Concord.* N194

Waite, Robert G. L. *Vanguard of Nazism: The Free Corps Movement in Postwar Germany, 1918–1923.* N181

Warmington, B. H. *Nero: Reality and Legend.* N542

Warren, Harris Gaylord. *Herbert Hoover and the Great Depression.* N394

Wedgwood, C. V. *William the Silent.* N185

Wheeler-Bennett, John W. *Brest-Litovsk: The Forgotten Peace, March 1918.* N576

Wolfers, Arnold. *Britain and France between Two Wars.* N343

Wolff, Robert Lee. *The Balkans in Our Time.* N395

Wright, Benjamin Fletcher. *Consensus and Continuity, 1776–1787.* N402

Zeldin, Theodore. *The Political System of Napoleon III.* N580

Zinn, Howard. *LaGuardia in Congress.* N488

Zobel, Hiller B. *The Boston Massacre.* N606